ANNUAL 1978

CONTENTS

© IPC Magazine
S.B.N. 8503

D0419068

25

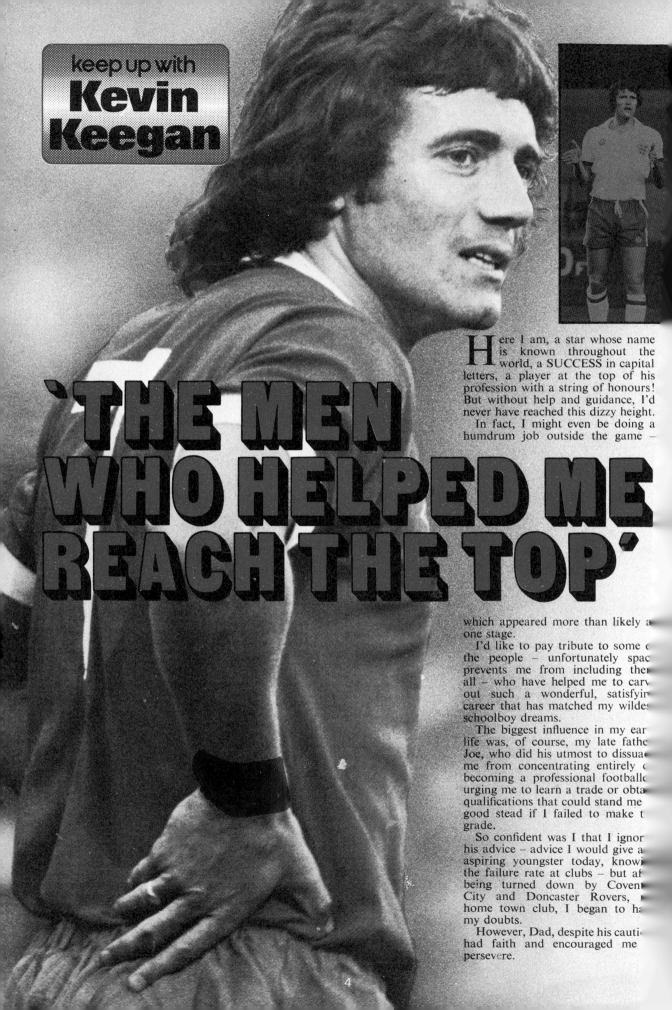

keep up with Kevin Keegan

'THE MEN WHO HELPED ME REACH THE TOP'

Here I am, a star whose name is known throughout the world, a SUCCESS in capital letters, a player at the top of his profession with a string of honours! But without help and guidance, I'd never have reached this dizzy height.

In fact, I might even be doing a humdrum job outside the game – which appeared more than likely a one stage.

I'd like to pay tribute to some of the people – unfortunately spac prevents me from including ther all – who have helped me to carv out such a wonderful, satisfyir career that has matched my wildes schoolboy dreams.

The biggest influence in my ear life was, of course, my late fathe Joe, who did his utmost to dissua me from concentrating entirely becoming a professional footballe urging me to learn a trade or obta qualifications that could stand me good stead if I failed to make t grade.

So confident was I that I ignor his advice – advice I would give a aspiring youngster today, knowi the failure rate at clubs – but af being turned down by Covent City and Doncaster Rovers, home town club, I began to ha my doubts.

However, Dad, despite his cauti had faith and encouraged me persevere.

4

He'd come along to watch me play. Unlike some misguided fathers, though, he didn't run along the touchline yelling out a constant stream of advice, trying to play my game for me. He realised I had to do it on my own.

Then into my life came Bob Nellis, a larger-than-life character, who I so impressed while playing against him in a Sunday League game he asked if I was interested in going for a trial with Scunthorpe United with a view to signing junior forms for them.

I jumped at the opportunity. Sure enough, it proved a case of third time lucky and I joined The Irons, playing for the youth team under the direction of Geoff Barker, chief scout.

The Old Show Ground was 25 miles away, and the problem of getting there for home games was solved by Bob dropping me off by car.

Bob, a furniture salesman, collected payments from customers on his way so it meant a different route every time!

Bob is also a great follower of the oval ball game, and is now chairman of Doncaster Rugby League club. I'll never forget how he helped get me started in football.

The next big influence on me was Ron Ashman, Scunthorpe manager, who rejoined the club in 1975 for another spell. Older readers will recall that Ron once hit the headlines as a member of a Norwich City side, then in the Third Division, which reached the Semi-Final of the F.A. Cup in 1958–59.

Ron is a sensitive man who cares about people. It's made him many friends, but has probably proved a handicap in his career. No manager can be so considerate to everyone and achieve success, unfortunately.

He always did what was best for me – bringing me into the first-team at 17 and dropping me for games against very physical, fierce-tackling sides to avoid the risk of my being kicked out of football. I was still very frail and also hadn't learnt to jump as though competing in the Horse of the Year Show!

When I was 19 he gave me my first taste of responsibility by appointing me captain, in preference to older and more experienced men in the side.

Around this clubs time several more illustrious clubs came to look me over, but cither they lost interest or their bids were too low.

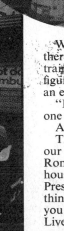

Three managers Kevin played under, and who helped shape him into one of the world's greatest players: England boss Don Revie (top, with Mike Doyle and Trevor Brooking), Ron Ashman (above), and the former Liverpool boss Bill Shankly (right). Below is George Best, whose off-field activities made Kevin wary of the high life.

Whenever I got disheartened, there was Jack Brownsword, our trainer, another sort of "father figure" to me, who like my Dad was an ex-miner, to keep my spirits up.

"Don't worry, you'll be a big name one day, Kev-lad," he'd say.

And I thought he was kidding!

Then, on the Friday evening after our last game of the 1970–71 season, Ron Ashman called round to my house with the big news – "The Press have got hold of it, Kev, so I think it's only fair to tell you, before you read it in the newspapers, that Liverpool want you to go there on

(continued on page 6)

Monday to discuss terms with them!"

I was over the moon, as they say. Wanted by Liverpool – one of the biggest, most glamorous clubs in Britain, in Europe!

Ron was just as excited for me.

He accompanied me to Anfield, a hive of activity not because I was signing for them – at £33,000 I was hardly a big buy – but because the club was preparing to play Arsenal in the 1971 F.A. Cup Final at Wembley.

It was nice to have Ron to help me with all my personal arrangements.

The joy of joining Liverpool was tinged with regret at leaving a club where I'd made so many good friends – Ron and Jack, the directors and, last but by no means least, the fans.

The man who helped me to make the transition, Liverpool's then-

Kevin soars above a Finland defender during last seasons' World Cup-tie at Wembley.

manager Bill Shankly, is without question the person to whom I'm most in debt. Shanks built-up my confidence, put me in the first-team without my ever having played a competitive game for the Central League side. He inspired me.

He has this knack of lifting players, bringing the best out of them.

Shanks is renowned for his witty remarks and outrageous comments.

I'm always telling my favourite story about him.

I was in the Anfield dressing-room before my eighth or ninth game for Liverpool. West Ham were our opponents and I was about to face that great defender Bobby Moore. Shanks must have sensed my tension. He came over and said: "Aye, I've just seen the West Ham team get off their coach. Bobby Moore is limping

– looks scared to death. Go at him, son. Run rings round him."

Of course, I didn't really believe it. But his pep talk relaxed me. I went out and helped The Reds to a 3–1 win.

Afterwards, Shanks came in grinning all over his craggy face. 'Well played, son. What did I tell you about Bobby Moore? Didn't put a foot wrong, did he? A g-r-e-a-t player!"

What a con-man! But a loveable, generous character who did so much for me.

After Shanks had resigned, Bob Paisley came out from under the great man's shadow and showed that he can achieve as much in his own fashion.

Bob is very different from Shanks – much quieter, more thoughtful, but held in similar respect and affection.

We have several things in common.

For instance, he knows my background, as he was born in Hetton-le-Hole, the same village as my Dad, and being a former Liverpool player he understands the pressures and problems that beset me.

Bob is magic at the treatment of injuries, one of his jobs as the former trainer.

It's true to say that the honours that came our way after he became manager, we won mainly for him.

In my international career I have to thank two men, Joe Mercer and Don Revie, for their tolerance and guidance.

I only played two games under Sir Alf Ramsey. Consequently, I did not get close to him, like the members of the World Cup-winning side.

Joe Mercer, as genial as his reputation says he is, believed in me, giving me seven games while care-taker-manager before Don Revie took the England post.

At first I was wary of "The Rev" simply because as boss of Leeds, our biggest rivals for many seasons, he had represented "the enemy".

I was soon won over, especially when he forgave me for quitting the England H.Q. before a match with Wales. I had misguidedly taken offence on learning I wasn't in the team, instead of waiting for him to explain that he was saving me for the next game, the really big one, against Scotland at Wembley.

Once he realised my main aim in life is to play for England – and in *every* game – he couldn't do enough for me, appointing me captain on several occasions.

Among the players I have learnt a great deal from are Bobby Moore and George Best.

Mooro, who must be included in any Hall of Fame of British Foot-ballers, steered me away from many of the off-field pitfalls, particularly in the business world, that lay in wait for me.

A lesser man would not have admitted his mistakes.

George Best taught me by obser-vation how not to get caught up in the high life of night clubs, etc.

If up-and-coming youngsters come into contact with such company as the men I've singled out they will be fortunate indeed.

And if those stars of tomorrow select me as someone who helped shape their careers, I'll feel I've ploughed at least something back into the game that has given me the good life.

Kevin Keegan

Liverpool manager Bob Paisley with (from left): Emlyn Hughes, Tommy Smith, Ian Callaghan, Terry McDermott and Phil Thomp-son. Kevin likes and respects Bob.

SPOT THE DIFFERENCE

"Off!" shouts the ref. But Fido's enjoying himself too much. While we're waiting for
our artist has made 20 alterations.

8

SPOT THE DIFFERENCE

the game to re-start, compare the drawing on the left with the one on the right, to which
Solution on page 125.

9

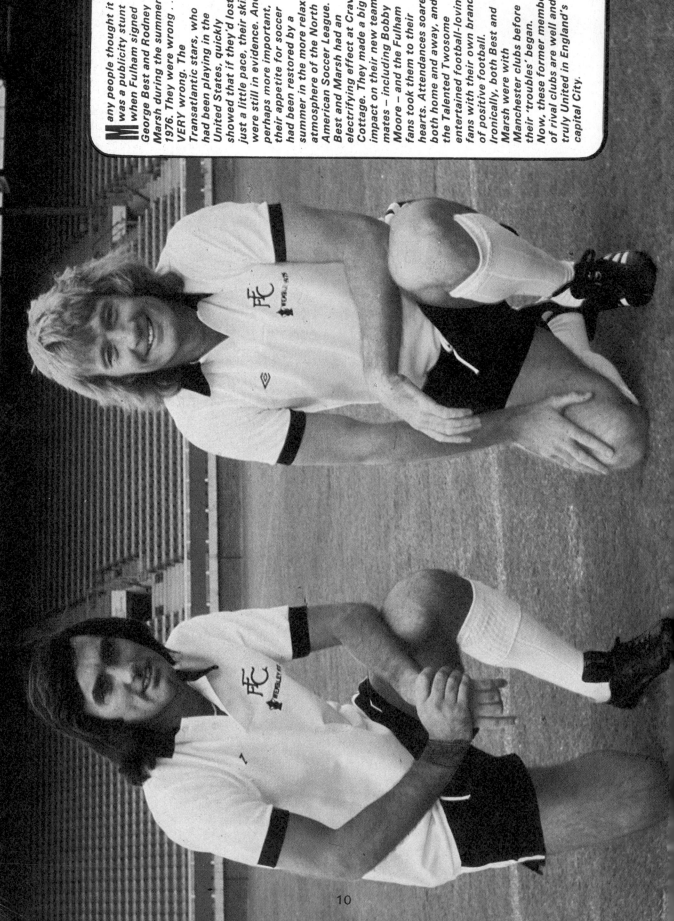

Many people thought it was a publicity stunt when Fulham signed George Best and Rodney Marsh during the summer of 1976. They were wrong . . . VERY wrong. The Transatlantic stars, who had been playing in the United States, quickly showed that if they'd lost just a little pace, their skills were still in evidence. And, perhaps more important, their appetite for soccer had been restored by a summer in the more relaxed atmosphere of the North American Soccer League. Best and Marsh had an electrifying effect at Craven Cottage. They made a big impact on their new team-mates – including Bobby Moore – and the Fulham fans took them to their hearts. Attendances soared, both home and away, and the Talented Twosome entertained football-loving fans with their own brand of positive football. Ironically, both Best and Marsh were with Manchester clubs before their 'troubles' began. Now, these former members of rival clubs are well and truly United in England's capital City.

11

STORY OF A STAR
ALEX STEPNEY

A GREAT 'KEEPER

Alex began his career with amateurs Tooting and Mitcham before signing professional for Millwall in May, 1963, at the age of 20.

A week before his and United's European Cup triumph, Alex made his first appearance for England against Sweden at Wembley. It turned out to be a happy debut as England won 3–1 with goals by Martin Peters, Bobby Charlton and Roger Hunt.

Following their relegation from the First Division in 1974, Manchester United bounced back at the first attempt when they were crowned Second Division Champions. Alex helps captain Martin Buchan to carry the trophy.

Almost three years to the day later, Stepney moved to Chelsea for £50,000. Here he watches first-choice 'keeper Peter Bonetti in a work-out. After just one League game in four months he moved to Manchester United in September, 1966, for around £53,000.

In his first season at Old Trafford, Alex collected a League Championship medal (left). And the following year was a member of the United team that beat Benfica 4–1 at Wembley to win the European Cup.

United battled to the 1976 F.A. Cup Final and were one of the hottest favourites ever. But, against all the odds, were beaten 1–0 by Second Division Southampton. Alex looks on in despair as Bobby Stokes' superbly-placed shot beats his valiant dive.

Today, Alex Stepney is one of the top goal-keepers in the country. His safe handling and acrobatic saves have thrilled fans since his debut 14 years ago.

SOCCER THE U.S.A. WAY

Soccer has slowly but very surely taken off in the United States.

Soccer – not football, as over there football means American football.

The 1976 Bicentennial Cup competition, won by Brazil, was a huge success and the Americans showed they are capable of staging a big soccer tournament.

Our pictures capture the pre-match atmosphere of the American game.

Bands and dancing girls make it a carnival occasion.

On the right, is Pele, whose transfer to the New York Cosmos soon after the 1974 World Cup Finals set the North American Soccer League alight.

Here, the Brazilian ace is in action for Team America in the Bicentennial Cup game against England . . . he prepares to take on Trevor Cherry.

Go For The Double

After solving the clues in this specially compiled crossword, you can use the letters in the thick-edged squares to form the name of a Liverpool and England defender. Answers on page 31.

ACROSS:
- (1) Geoff –, Bristol City defender.
- (6) Stenhous – – – ir.
- (9) Har – lep – – –, from Victoria Ground.
- (11) Trevor Franc – – of Birmingham City.
- (12) Cardiff City's ground. (6 & 4)
- (16) Trevor Ta – n – on of Bristol City.
- (17) Jimmy C – – d – rwood of Birmingham.
- (18) Submissive – the opposite of most players!
- (20) West Germ – – –, 1974 World Cup Winners.
- (21) Room between two players, for instance.
- (22) An old measurement of length needed to complete Barry Pow – – – of Coventry.
- (24) John Pr – – t of Spurs.
- (25) – – – ffield United from Bramall Lane.
- (26) Sammy –, Arsenal full-back.
- (29) Fuel from the missing letters in Len – – nte – l – of West Bromwich Albion.
- (30) Jimm – Neighb – – – of Norwich City.
- (31) Jimmy –, Bristol City player.
- (32) – Bowles, Queens Park Rangers striker.
- (33) – Baxter, former famous name with Rangers and Scotland.
- (34) – – rwich, from Carrow Road.
- (37) Notts County play at – – ad – w – a – e. A citrus fruit from the missing letters.
- (38) Chris –, Aston Villa defender.

DOWN:
- (1) David –, Leeds United striker.
- (2) Move at a faster rate than walking.
- (3) World Cup Winners in 1934 and 1938.
- (4) Keith – – l – ma – of West Ham. A shape from the missing letters.
- (5) The Liverpool crowd!
- (7) Southampton and England striker. (4 & 7)
- (8) Stewart Ho – – ton of Manchester United.
- (10) Frank – – – – ard of West Ham.
- (13) Frank McL – n – ock of Q.P.R.
- (14) – Mellor, Brighton player.
- (15) Justification or motive.
- (19) Kevin – – – – an, Norwich goalkeeper.
- (20) Club third in Scottish Second Division in 1975–76 season.
- (21) Ian – John, Portsmouth manager.
- (23) – Stadium, home of Orient.
- (24) M – – or Road Ground, home of Oxford.
- (27) Alan – – – derland of Wolves.
- (28) Peter St – – ey of Arsenal.
- (29) O – dha – – thl – ti –. An animal from the missing letters.
- (31) Field –, Mansfield Town's ground.
- (35) Roger Keny – – of Everton.
- (36) St. J – – nstone!

Laugh Away

'Hello! Another economy cut! They've replaced our coach'

'I had it built for away matches – it carries twelve'

'Someone's boobed! Our Liverpool team has travelled down to Upton Park'

'Ever since the club paid out £400,000 for glamour boy downstairs . . .'

CROSSTALK How have goal-

Alan Gowling (stripes, left) scores Newcastle's goal in the 1976 League Cup Final against Manchester City.

'Nowadays, there is little space to operate in near goal' – Alan Gowling – goal-menace of the Seventies

In the days of the 2-3-5 formation and spearhead centre-forwards, Stan Mortensen of Blackpool and England was one of football's greatest match-winners. So when we decided to compare goal-getting in the Fifties to goal-scoring today we sought Mortensen's views – and also the opinion of Newcastle United's ace marksman, Alan Gowling, on whether strikers have a tougher job in the Seventies than they did 25 years ago. Here, both men discuss the ability and flair required to be successful forwards then and now – and as goal-scoring has been important in any era, what Stan and Alan have to say is well worth noting!

Gowling: The players of 25 years ago would find it much harder to score nowadays. Modern defenders are fitter and faster, and the tactics they use make it difficult for a forward to break through.

Mortensen: I can't agree with that, Alan. I don't deny that modern training methods have produced fitter players – but where are your fast men today? We had speed merchants such as Joe Hulme, Frank Broome and Jackie Milburn in the past, and I think the game has slowed down since their day.

Gowling: I admit you had some fast individual players, Stan, including yourself. But today, everything is geared to make the game as a whole quicker than it was. Passing, running into position and covering is done at a much quicker tempo.

Mortensen: The covering was also good when I played. As a centre-forward I always had a centre-half on my back, and he had a man behind him to back him up. But we were never afraid to take on a couple of defenders, whereas today the forwards seem frightened of responsibility – they are usually looking for a colleague to pass to and to give them a helping hand.

Gowling: The modern game certainly gives less opportunity for individualism. For example, that great winger Stan Matthews would not be given much scope today – he made goal-scoring easier for centre-forwards by creating openings which we would seal off.

Mortensen: Yes, Stan and other wingmen made openings for us, and he often beat two or three men in the process. But we still had to put the ball in the back of the net – and remember that the old-fashioned ball was much heavier than today's version. How many forwards today could whack that heavy ball past the goalkeeper from 30 or 40 yards as we frequently did?

Gowling: Agreed, Stan, the old-type ball would have presented problems to us and made goal-scoring harder – but we could overcome this by practise with a heavy ball. Could old-time centre-forwards have overcome a modern defence with four men at the back?

Mortensen: Men in the Forties and Fifties, such as Tommy Lawton, Nat Lofthouse and others were very talented goalscorers. With their talent, they would get goals at any period in soccer history, including the 1970's.

Gowling: Nobody would deny that – but goalscoring charts of today show less goals are being scored now. And even Lawton and Lofthouse would find it hard.

Mortensen: The reason for fewer goals being scored is due to the fact that there is hardly a centre-

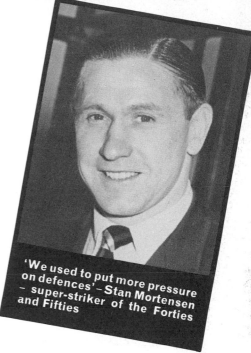

'We used to put more pressure on defences' – Stan Mortensen – super-striker of the Forties and Fifties

as well today as they used to, except on a rare occasion. And teams manage to score goals without them.

Mortensen: There is one type of goal that we regularly got that is much more uncommon today – this is the headed goal at the near post, which is harder to score than one at the far post. It takes courage to get a near-post goal. More than is needed to sneak up behind a defence.

Gowling: You old-timers had courage, Stan – you needed it to head that heavy ball! And you had talent – but you would find that it is harder to show polished ball-control in a game in which everything happens at top speed.

Mortensen: Good footballers can operate at any speed, Alan. When I was manager at Blackpool I advised players like Tony Green and Tommy Hutchison to make a point of beating men, and no matter how packed a defence is, a first-class player can do it – and score goals.

Gowling: In the game of 25 years ago, I think there were far more situations in which a centre-forward could score goals. Nowadays, there is very little space to operate in near goal, and you would have found this a problem.

Mortensen: It would not be easy. Yet we were much more ready to shoot from long distances than the modern forward is, and I'm sure an old-type centre-forward would enjoy shooting with the light modern ball. But we were also good finishers from close range, and our football was more exciting to watch.

Gowling: Yes, because a lot of it was played off the cuff, and modern tactics would prevent this.

forward around who will run at defences. Malcolm Macdonald is probably the only one who reminds me of a typical centre-forward.

Gowling: I don't believe that running at a modern defence would get the results it did against a rearguard in the Fifties. Teams are more concentrated at the back today.

Mortensen: We used to put more pressure on defences, Alan, and defenders were really tested. Take today's centre-halves – forwards run away from them, whereas we ran directly at defenders at top speed and this unsettled them. In addition, full-backs have few wingers to contend with, so their weaknesses are not often exposed.

Gowling: I know that arguments about whether to bring back wingers can provide a great talking-point, but I don't think they would function

Mortensen: Whatever the reason, our football was more attractive to watch, Alan – football should be a presentation, the sort that attracts the crowds. At Blackpool we often had 40,000 gates.

Gowling: Well, Stan, there are still well-supported teams. The difficult part about any discussion involving players of quarter of a century ago and today is that our arguments are impossible to prove. I reckon the only thing we can really agree on beyond doubt is the fact that modern training techniques are superior to the old.

Mortensen: When I think of the constant lapping we did round the track at Bloomfield, I have to say that our training lacked imagination. Yet somehow, even with those old-fashioned football boots, we were quick off the mark.

Gowling: I suppose natural speed and talent are both something a player is born with, and these assets would make up for lack of tip-top training. And great goal-getters in any era, such as Jimmy Greaves at his best, and Malcolm Macdonald today, had short strides that gave them rapid movement in the penalty area.

Mortensen: And lastly, finishing ability – this would have got you some goals against teams in my day, Alan, and I hope would have given me some against your modern defences. So perhaps this argument can end in a draw . . .

Stan Mortensen (second right) in action for Blackpool against Bolton Wanderers in the 1953 F.A. Cup Final.

19

What the game is all about G·O·A·L·S!

TOP OF PAGE . . . Martin Dobson (dark shirt) beats a Bristol City defender to head a goal for Everton.
ABOVE . . . The Orient defence is stranded as Malcolm Smith scores for Burnley.
RIGHT . . . Dave Clement, the Queens Park Rangers full-back, slams the ball past Aston Villa's Chris Nicholl – and a goal is just a second away!
FAR RIGHT . . . Leeds United striker David McNiven is well placed to steer home this goal against Newcastle United at Elland Road.

ABOVE, RIGHT . . . Kenny Burns of Birmingham scores his fourth goal against Derby in 1976-77 at St. Andrews.

RIGHT . . . The deadly left foot of Liverpool's Steve Heighway is too good for Norwich on this occasion.

NEWS DESK

Compiled by PETER STEWART

CELTIC — England's Champions?

Old mates

It was almost home-from-home when Scotland Under-23 defender Gordon Smith arrived at Villa Park from St. Johnstone last season. There in the first-team squad was his old chum Andy Gray.

Both come from the same district in Glasgow and often travelled to training together when Andy was at Dundee United as the grounds – Saints and United's – are only about 20 miles apart.

They also played in the same Scotland Under-23 team against Denmark in October, 1975.

Goalkeepers don't exactly make the most successful Football League club managers.

Believe it or not, only one has led a club to a major honour: Gil Merrick, when Birmingham City won the Football League Cup in 1962-63.

Mind you, there have been only 19 goalkeepers in charge of clubs since the Second World War – so perhaps the record isn't as bad as it appears.

Just how would the glorious Celtic team which won the European Cup in 1967 have fared in England?

That is a question which still provokes arguments between Scottish and English fans.

One man in no doubt that Celtic then could have ruled England is Bobby Murdoch, midfield-master of The Lisbon Lions, shown being crowned after the big event by team-mates Tommy Gemmell and John Clark.

"That team wouldn't have just won the English League title that year – it would have won it for at least the next two seasons," declares Bobby.

"I have no hesitation in saying that because Celtic at the time were a truly great team. Once every lifetime you get a club where everything blends on and off the field and at all levels.

"That is why we were just about unbeatable, especially under a great manager like Jock Stein, and I'm sure none of the English teams could have stopped us."

But Bobby knows that English fans are often sceptical about Scottish teams, and that is why he is glad he went to Middlesbrough after being granted a free transfer by Celtic in recognition of his services.

Many judges felt that Boro boss Jackie Charlton – then pushing for promotion – had scooped one of the bargains of the century.

So it proved . . . for Bobby's skill and experience played a major role in helping Boro romp out of Division Two and more than establish themselves in the top flight.

But what differences did Bobby find between the English and Scottish Leagues?

"English teams place more emphasis on team work – and I think they also work harder. Scottish players, though, still have more flair.

"But in the English First Division every game is hard, whereas with Celtic we knew we could win several games each season without too much trouble.

"Mind you, that doesn't mean I'll change my mind over my claim that the 1967 Celtic side could have been Champions of England!"

Scoring full-back partners

It's not often a team's full-backs both get on the scoresheet in the same match, but it happened last season when Ces Podd and Peter Hardcastle both found the net in Bradford City's 4-0 romp at Southport.

A particular red-letter day for Podd. It was his first goal for City and it came in his 200th first-team appearance.

Funnily enough, City's manager Bobby Kennedy was one of the last to share a similar feat. It was when he was playing for Manchester City against Bolton Wanderers in 1966.

Kennedy and his full-back partner Cliff Sear were both on target in a 4-1 triumph.

Others to have achieved this feat have been Trollope and Dawson for Swindon against Mansfield; Reaney and Hair for Leeds against Stoke; Brennan and Burns for Manchester United against Nottingham Forest; Parkin and Wilson for Wolves against Southampton; Cohen and Langley for Fulham against Brighton; Bircumshaw and Drysdale for Hartlepool against Barrow; and Rudman and Ferguson for Rochdale against Darlington.

Ted MacDougall's £50,000 move from Norwich City to Southampton last season brought the till ringing up to £585,000 on his travels which started at Liverpool ten years ago.

He cost York City £5,000, Bournemouth £10,000, Manchester United £220,000, West Ham £170,000 and Norwich £130,000.

The University College Dublin soccer club made history in September, 1976, by becoming the first European football team to visit Communist China.

Twenty-four players and four officials went on the tour to play games in Peking, Canton, and Shanghai, followed by matches in Bombay, Hong Kong and Thailand.

The trip cost the club £10,000 – and, apart from grants from the Football Association of Ireland and the Amateur Soccer League, the students raised the money themselves over two years by holding socials and staging games.

A super-bike for Super-Mac. Arsenal and England striker Malcolm Macdonald gets the feel of the Triumph Bonneville 750, which has a top speed of 110 mph and does around 50 miles to the gallon.

Supermac can't possibly match figures like that, even though at £333,000 he did cost almost 300 times more than the price of a Bonneville.

Sheffield United winger Chico Hamilton played in all four Divisions of the Football League before he was 20. He started with Southend in the Fourth, and played in all the other three Divisions with Aston Villa before his move to Bramall Lane during the summer of 1976.

● Of the 14 League of Ireland clubs, only three of them have proper floodlighting systems. Bohemians' Dalymount Park in Dublin, Home Farm's Tolka Park, also in Dublin, and Dundalk's Oriel Park.

Keegan of Coventry

Guess what these players have in common. Kevin Keegan, Ray Clemence, Mick Mills, Kevin Beattie, Colin Bell, Ian Gillard, Tony Currie and John Radford.

Answer – they all had trials with other Football League clubs and were turned down.

Otherwise, you could have been reading about Keegan of Coventry, Clemence of Notts County, Mills of Portsmouth, Beattie of Liverpool, Bell of Huddersfield, Gillard of Tottenham Hotspur, Currie of Chelsea and Radford of Bradford City.

'PRESSURES — RUBBISH' declares Charlton boss

If there's one thing Charlton manager Andy Nelson (above) can't stand it's footballers who talk of pressure.

"It makes me sick to hear a player moan about there being too many matches in a season.

"It's no harder than when I was a player, and it's still a good life. After all, you're playing a game you enjoy otherwise you wouldn't be there in the first place.

"We used to love having two games a week, and that's the best way of keeping match fit.

"If anyone feels it's all too much for him he ought to get out."

● Before the 1914-18 War, the Football League season always began on 1st September on whatever day it fell, apart from Friday and Sunday. And it always ended on 30th April.

● Arsenal are building quite an Irish colony at Highbury, led, of course, by manager Terry Neill. But they haven't caught up with the old Leeds City club of the early 1900's, who had no fewer than 12 Irishmen on their books at one time.

● Stoke City's Denis Smith must surely rank as the most unluckiest player in the game. He has broken a leg four times and his nose five times.

Well-paid men of Stirling

Who are the highest-paid footballers in Scotland? Obviously those with Rangers and Celtic.

But the part-timers of ambitious Stirling Albion, with smart offices and a well-appointed pavilion, do as well as some of the top players with the Old Firm.

Stirling boss Alex Smith has said that some of his men earn around £70 a week from their everyday jobs and then collect a sizeable cheque from the club for their services.

"In fact," said Mr. Smith, "I'm pretty sure there will be some players at Parkhead and Ibrox who are not as well off as our lads."

No, not a substitute enjoying a half-time cup of tea, but one of the TV chimps which entertained the Bristol City crowd before their League match against West Ham last season.

'The best of SUPER-SAM is yet to come'

Manchester United striker Sammy McIlroy (left) became so frustrated with his lack of goal-scoring form early last season that he asked his boss Tommy Docherty to drop him from the first-team.

But Belfast-born Sammy's shock request was flatly refused by The Doc, who ordered the Northern Ireland star to: "Go out on the park and play your way back to form!"

Much-travelled Docherty has made no secret of the fact that he rates Sammy McIlroy very highly, and has gone on record as saying: "In my view we have yet to see the best of our brilliant, world-class Super-Sam."

Although a Football League regular for several seasons, the United star is still only 23 and looks set for a long and successful playing career.

There's an odd coincidence between the two men who've given the longest unbroken service to League clubs.

Newcastle director Stan Seymour and Southampton chairman George Reeder both began their careers with their respective clubs as forwards – and both made their League debuts in 1920-21.

We wonder if there are any strikers around today who'll be with the same clubs in the year 2032?

'Why I like Liverpool' ANDY KING, Everton

Andy King, signed by Everton for £40,000 from Luton in March, 1976, has a special regard for Merseyside.

"It still amazes me that Everton came in for me," says Andy. "It made me feel very proud, and equalled the moment when I went on as sub for Luton in a First Division match at Liverpool. The area has always had happy memories for me."

'I couldn't justify my record fee'

says Derby's DAVID NISH

At £225,000, Derby County's David Nish is still Britain's most expensive full-back.

Former Rams manager Brian Clough gave Nish the "honour" when he paid that huge sum to Leicester City in 1972.

The subsequent slump in the transfer market makes it likely that Nish will remain our costliest full-back for a long while. Managers are reluctant to pay big money for defenders, even though they are every bit as important as the goal-getters.

Nish is used to his price-tag now, but owns up to being rather worried at first.

He reasons: "How could I justify my fee? I couldn't really be expected to score a hatful of goals.

"At the same time, I rarely had a chance to make the final 'killer' pass that led to a goal.

"All I could do was to go out and play my natural game.

"I used to play in midfield so I have always liked to attack. I just got on with my main job of defending.

"There are problems for a new player whatever the fee. He has to prove himself to the fans and his team-mates. They want to be assured he will boost the side.

"But a bad pass when you cost over £200,000 brings more nasty remarks than if you cost a fraction of it."

Nish's debut for Derby was at Carrow Road against Norwich City and he admits to being "scared stiff".

He continues: "I was worried not so much for myself, but the team. I wanted us to win . . . I was not particularly concerned how I played myself.

"Having a blinder and being on the losing side is no consolation."

That, in fact, was the story of Nish's debut as The Canaries snatched victory.

There was another problem for Nish. Derby, as Champions, were in the European Cup, but he was not eligible until the later rounds.

"It was dreadful to have to drop out for the European ties," he says.

"The lads were doing really well, especially to beat Benfica 3-0.

"Then, when I came back for League matches, the sparkle was missing. I began to wonder if I could ever regain my form.

Perfectionist

"Losing to Juventus in the Semi-Finals was a choker. We just didn't get a break in Turin and at home we had the chances to win, but didn't take them."

Nish is a worrier. Perhaps perfectionist would be a better word. He feels deeply about football . . . and about Derby County.

When Clough bought him, The Rams got more than just an expensive full-back.

They got a quietly-spoken star with the tenacity of a tiger who takes defeat as a personal insult.

It has surprised many knowledgeable soccer folk that Nish does not have more than five England caps to his credit.

After all, England haven't exactly been blessed with full-backs in recent years and Don Revie has tried various combinations without really finding a top-class blend.

Perhaps it's because Nish is not a publicity-seeker. He prefers to let his football do the talking and in this respect he certainly can't be ignored!

Tottenham Hotspur fans must be amongst the luckiest in Britain. Over the years, they've been entertained by some of the greatest names in our soccer history . . . Greaves, Blanchflower, Mackay, White . . . to name just four.

Now, another player seems destined to stand alongside the greats in the Spurs Hall of Fame . . . Glenn Hoddle.

Unlike many of the famous stars of White Hart Lane, Hoddle is home-produced.

As a youngster, he used to idolise The Lilywhites from the terraces – now, it's his turn to be admired by what have been described as the most critical supporters in the League.

Maybe, but if that's the case then it says much for Hoddle that he was a favourite from the word "go".

This is his third season in League football and the confidence he shows is beyond his tender years.

Hoddle's first first-team appearance did not cause too much of a stir.

It was against Norwich City at White Hart Lane in the early part of 1975-76 when he came on as substitute, aged just 17.

He says: "I did not expect to be given a chance so early, but having got a taste for the big-time I quickly raised my standards.

"No longer did I want to be a promising reserve or substitute. I wanted to be where it mattered – in the League team."

"Home-Grown"

Hoddle's first full game for Spurs raised more eyebrows. It was at Stoke later in that season and he scored a goal that even Jimmy Greaves himself would have been proud of.

As luck would have it, the television cameras were at the Victoria Ground . . . and a new star was born.

Hoddle has matured rapidly. In 1976-77 he established himself in the first-team, and week after week was given "man of the match" ratings by newspapers.

He says: "In 1975-76, I was in and out of the side. Terry Neill was the manager and I think he was wary of over-exposing me.

"To be honest, even though I was very young, I was disappointed when I wasn't included. Age shouldn't come into it . . . it's what a player does on the park that counts, whether he is 17 or 37.

"When Keith Burkinshaw took over in 1976, I vowed that I'd make it hard for him to leave me out.

"I worked on all aspects of my game, especially tackling. Although I'm not a defender, I must be involved when I've not got the ball and must share some defensive duties."

Hoddle, one of the brightest stars seen in London for ages, is not tempted by the distractions offered by the capital.

"Basically, I live the same sort of life as I did when I was an apprentice.

"I like going to the pictures during the week. On Saturdays, I might have a drink with my mates, but other than that I'm not worried about the so-called good life."

Believe it or not, Hoddle is not far short of his TENTH anniversary at White Hart Lane.

"I began going along for training when I was about 11. This was a dream come true for me. I was Spurs mad.

"When they asked me to sign apprentice forms, I hesitated for a while. Spurs had a reputation for playing big-fee players rather than their own stars.

"But all this has changed over the years. Several younger players have made their mark and there is a new era starting at the club."

One that will surely show Glenn Hoddle as a "home-grown" star worthy of a place alongside the best.

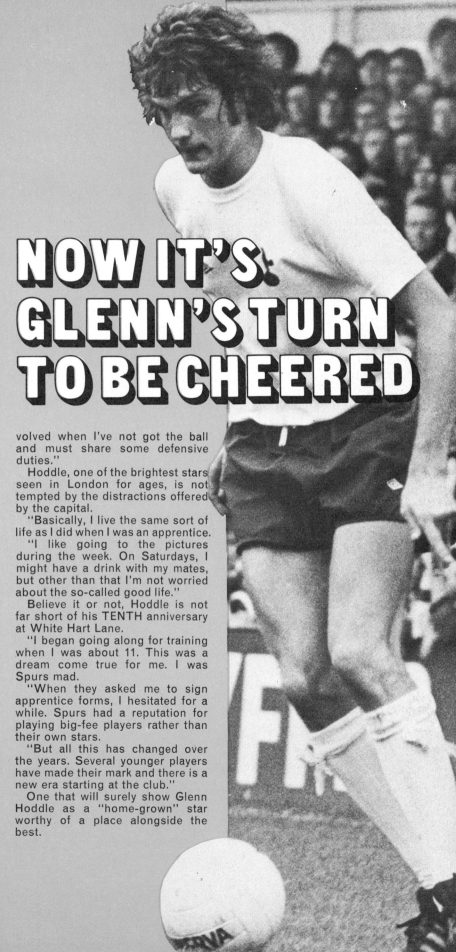

NOW IT'S GLENN'S TURN TO BE CHEERED

LEFT . . . 10-goal Joe Payne of Luton Town.

of at least 42 games – 21 goals, Southampton, 42 games, Third Division (S), 1921-22, and also Port Vale, 46 games, Third Division (N), 1953-54.

● The highest score by an individual in a Football League game – 10 goals by Joe Payne, Luton Town v. Bristol Rovers, Third Division (S), April 13th, 1936. A reserve half-back, this was Payne's first appearance in the League as a centre-forward.

● The greatest winning margin by a Football League Championship-winning team – Preston North End 1888-89, Sunderland 1892-93, Aston Villa 1896-97, and Manchester United 1955-56, each finished 11 points ahead of their nearest rivals.

● In season 1946-47 Doncaster Rovers won the Championship of Third Division (N) with a record 33 wins in 42 games. They also notched up the highest number of away wins ever attained – 18 out of 21, helping to give them an all-time record bag of 37 away points. Despite these achievements, however, they were relegated the following season.

● Millwall had created a Football League record with a run of 59 home games without defeat before Plymouth came to The Den and

run in Third Division.

● 14 wins in a row is a Football League record that was first set up by Bristol City in 1905-06 and equalled by Preston North End in 1950-51. Both clubs were in Second Division.

● Leeds United played 29 First Division games in season 1973-74 before suffering their first defeat – 2-3 at Stoke. This is a record start to a season equalled only by Liverpool in season 1893-94, but their achievement was slightly different. The Reds won all 28 of the season's Second Division games and followed this by winning their Test match – played in those days to decide promotion and relegation.

● The longest run without defeat in the Football League in a single season is one of 30 games by Burnley in First Division in 1920-21.

● The smallest number of defeats in a season of at least 42 games is two by Leeds United in First Division, 1968-69. They were beaten 1-3 at Maine Road and 1-5 at Burnley.

● Liverpool won the Football League Championship in season 1965-66 with only 14 players – a record. But for the inclusion of Bobby Graham in only one game the

It's a record!

The highest score by one side in a Football League game is 13 goals – Stockport County 13, Halifax Town 0, January 6th, 1934; Tranmere Rovers 13, Oldham Athletic 4, December 26th, 1935, both games in Third Division (N); and Newcastle United 13, Newport County 0, in Second Division October 5th, 1946.

● The highest score away from home is Sheffield United's 10-0 victory on a snow-covered pitch at Burslem Port Vale, Second Division, December 10th, 1892. United scored four goals in the first six minutes.

● Most goals in a season – 134 by Peterborough United in 46 games, Fourth Division, 1960-61. The individual record is 60 by W. R. "Dixie" Dean (Everton) in 39 First Division games, 1927-28.

● Best defensive record in a season

MANCHESTER UNITED 1955-56.

beat them 2-1, January 14th, 1967.

● Huddersfield Town enjoyed a record run of 18 away Football League games without defeat between losing 0-1 at Bolton on November 15th, 1924, and 0-3 at Villa Park on November 14th, 1925. This was in the First Division.

● A run of 11 games without conceding a goal is a Football League record. Millwall first achieved this in Third Division (S) in 1925-26, and it was not equalled until 1973-74 when York City enjoyed a similar

total would have been 13, a remarkable figure which speaks volumes for the team's consistency. The 13 men (apperances in brackets) were – Lawrence (42); Lawler (40); Byrne (42); Milne (28) or Strong (21 + 1); Yeats (42); Stevenson (41); Callaghan (42); Hunt (37) or Arrowsmith (3 + 2); St. John (41); Smith (42); and Thompson (40).

● Because of crowd restrictions and the modernisation of many grounds a record that will never be beaten, unless a Football League game is played at Wembley, is the attendance record. There was a crowd of 83,260 at Maine Road when Manchester United met Arsenal in a First Division game, January 17th, 1948. United were then playing their home games at Maine Road while Old Trafford was being rebuilt after war damage.

FOOTBALL LEAGUE RECORDS THAT NOBODY WANTS TO BREAK

● In season 1898-99 Darwen conceded a record 141 goals in 34 Second Division games. Among their defeats were no less than three by margins of 10 goals, and three double-figure defeats in one season is another League record. No wonder that after that season Darwen were never seen again in the Football League.

● The greatest number of defeats in a season of League games is 33 by Rochdale in 40 games, Third Division (N), 1931-32.

● The smallest number of goals scored by a club in a season of at least 42 Football League games is 24 by Watford, Second Division, 1971-72. Keith Eddy was top scorer with six goals.

● Loughborough Town hit a record low with only one victory in 32 Second Division games, 1899-1900. Their tally of only eight points that

season (won 1, drawn 6) is another record, but this was equalled by Doncaster Rovers in 34 games, Second Division, 1904-05 (won 3, drawn 2).

● For a season of at least 42 games the record low is 17 points by Tranmere Rovers, 42 games, Second Division, 1938-39.

● Exeter City failed to score in their

Dixie Dean, the great Everton forward.

first 13 away games in Third Division (S), 1923-24. They broke their duck with a 1-0 win at Swindon on February 16th.

● Rochdale lost 17 games in succession in Third Division (N) in 1931-32. After beating New Brighton 3-2 on November 7th, 1931, they failed to gain another point until drawing 1-1 with the same opponents on March 9th, 1932.

● The longest run without a win in the Football League is one of 30 games by Crewe Alexandra in Third Division (N) in 1956-57.

● After winning 1-0 at Charlton on September 30th, 1922, Merthyr Town did not win another Third Division (S) game away from home until they gained a 2-0 victory at Swindon, September 19th, 1925.

Keith Eddy was Watford's top scorer in 1971-72 – with six goals!

Ron Yeats and Roger Hunt with the 1966 Charity Shield. The Reds won the Championship in 1965-66 using only 14 players.

'MY KIND OF PLAYER—'

By Bob Paisley, Liverpool manager

*L*iverpool's success for more than a decade has been built upon the Anfield club's outstanding ability to secure the right blend of players. And Bob Paisley, the Merseysiders' manager, holds emphatic views on what he looks for in men keen to don the red jersey.

"I must ask for character and skill to begin with in any player," says Mr. Paisley. "Also, he needs to have the ability to think quickly — these qualities are the basic attributes I want."

But in searching for players to fill the different positions in a team, the Liverpool boss is even more demanding.

GOALKEEPER

RAY CLEMENCE

A goalkeeper requires lightning-quick reflexes and courage to take risks, such as diving at the feet of an opposing forward. In addition he must be able to handle crosses expertly and able to deal with high and low shots.

"Then his positional sense in and around his goal-area ought to be first-class, and physically it is better if he is fairly tall."

FULL-BACK

In front of the goalkeeper, the modern full-back plays a different sort of game to the old-timer and is possibly a better all-round footballer. Instead of simply making a big clearance out of defence and considering his job ends there, the present-day back must be prepared to follow up with the play.

"He does this by overlapping on the flanks and in taking on the tasks of a winger to a certain extent. The full-back of the Seventies is much more attack-minded than his predecessor, but must also be equipped to tackle strongly when his side is under pressure."

PHIL NEAL

CENTRE-BACK

In the centre-back position, which is vital in any team's defensive set-up, Bob stresses good understanding between back-four men.

"The two centre-backs must work well together, with one taking the role of 'sweeper'. They should be able to read the game quickly and accurately, be good in the air, and ready to start off attacks.

"Added to which they have to mark tightly, and physical strength and height are useful here."

PHIL THOMPSON

RAY KENNEDY

MIDFIELDER

The engine-room of a side, the midfield area, calls for players with stamina, tackling ability and the knack of splitting defences with well-judged passes. Quickness of thought counts, and Pat Crerand, ex-Manchester United, proved that although he lacked pace on the ball his soccer brain made up for it.

"Some midfield men are expert at winning the ball, others have a flair for exploiting the weaknesses in opposing defences. The complete midfield player is able to do both."

And in the all-important goal-scoring department, the forward line, manager Paisley seeks a combination of talent which is directly aimed at putting the ball in the back of the net.

FORWARDS

A winger requires pace and the ability to take on defenders and his work on the flanks makes opportunities for himself and his colleagues.

"And the men who profit by the chances created by the rest of the team are the strikers – they have to possess goal sense, shooting power and speed. They receive plenty of knocks, and must be tough enough to accept them.

"Alongside the striker, or centre-forward is the forward who helps to probe defences and also score goals – Kevin Keegan does it for Liverpool and his job needs ball-control, a keen soccer brain and mobility.

"Then having got the right sort of ability in every department of the team, I make it my business to see that every man is prepared to work for his teammates. To be successful this spirit has to be developed, which is why I'm careful to select those players who give me this co-operation."

STEVE HEIGHWAY

SCORE A SOCCER CENTURY

Tackle this quiz, section by section, checking your answers with those printed upside down beneath each section. Award yourself two points for each correct answer. Then add up your scores and see how close you are to the maximum total of 100.

Transfers

The following players were all transferred during 1976-77. Their former clubs are in brackets . . . can you name the sides they joined?

1. Peter Taylor (Crystal Palace)
2. Ted MacDougall (Norwich)
3. Pat Howard (Newcastle)
4. Terry Yorath (Leeds)
5. Pat Stanton (Hibs)
6. Eddie Kelly (Arsenal)
7. John Connolly (Everton)
8. Alan Foggon (Manchester United)
9. Paul Went (Portsmouth)
10. Paul Mariner (Plymouth – below)

answers

1. Spurs; 2. Southampton; 3. Arsenal; 4. Coventry; 5. Celtic; 6. Q.P.R.; 7. Birmingham; 8. Sunderland; 9. Cardiff; 10. Ipswich.

True or False?

1. Bob Stokoe resigned as boss of Sunderland in October, 1976.
2. Mansfield Town play their home games at Vetch Field.
3. Nottingham Forest signed Terry Curran from Doncaster Rovers.
4. The 1976-77 Scottish League Cup Final was between Aberdeen and Celtic.
5. Rangers lost 5-1 to Celtic in the Semi-Finals of that competition.
6. George Best played his first League game for Fulham against Bristol Rovers last term.
7. Hereford's Terry Paine (above) holds the League appearance record.
8. Port Vale reached the 1954 F.A. Cup Final.
9. Last season was Bristol City's first in Division One since 1910-11.
10. Northern Ireland boss Danny Blanchflower represented his country 56 times.

answers

1. True; 2. False – they play at Field Mill; 3. True; 4. True; 5. False – Aberdeen beat Rangers 5-1; 6. True; 7. True; 8. False – they reached the Semi-Finals; 9. True; 10. True.

Nicknames

Internationals

Can you identify the clubs by their nicknames?
1. Red Imps
2. The Rams
3. Cottagers
4. Loons
5. Bankies
6. Terrors
7. The Seals
8. Killies
9. Rokerites
10. The Wee Rovers

answers

1. Lincoln City; 2. Derby County; 3. Fulham; 4. Forfar; 5. Clydebank; 6. Dundee United; 7. Chester; 8. Kilmarnock; 9. Sunderland; 10. Albion Rovers.

1976 Finals

Can you name the winners of the Cup Finals listed that were played during 1976?
1. European Championship (CHEZAS)
2. European Under-23 Championship (HUNGRAY)
3. European Super Cup (ADERLACHT)
4. European Cup (BAYREN MUNICH)
5. European Cup-Winners' Cup (ADERLACHT)
6. U.E.F.A. Cup (LIVERPOOL)
7. F.A. Cup (SOUTHAMPTON)
8. Football League Cup (below) (MAN. CITY)
9. Scottish Cup (RANGERS)
10. F.A. Challenge Trophy (SCADBROUGH)

answers

1. Czechoslovakia; 2. Hungary; 3. Anderlecht; 4. Bayern Munich; 5. Anderlecht; 6. Liverpool; 7. Southampton; 8. Manchester City; 9. Rangers; 10. Scarborough.

For which countries have the following Football League players played?
1. Chris Nicholl (Aston Villa)
2. Ken Burns (Birmingham)
3. Ray Wilkins (Chelsea – above)
4. Les Cartwright (Coventry)
5. Colin Viljoen (Ipswich)
6. Carl Harris (Leeds)
7. Willie Donachie (Manchester City)
8. Tony Grealish (Orient)
9. Ian Gillard (Q.P.R.)
10. Jimmy Johnstone (Sheffield United)

answers

1. N. Ireland; 2. Scotland; 3. England; 4. Wales; 5. England; 6. Wales; 7. Scotland; 8. Eire; 9. England; 10. Scotland.

GO FOR THE DOUBLE ANSWERS

Across: 1. Merrick; 6. Emu; 9. Tool; 11. Is; 12. Ninian Park; 16. It; 17. Ale; 18. Meek; 20. Any; 21. Space; 22. Ell; 24. At; 25. She; 26. Nelson; 29. Coal; 30. Your; 31. Mann; 32. Stan; 33. Jim; 34. No; 37. Lemon; 38. Nicholl.
Down: 1. McNiven; 2. Run; 3. Italy; 4. Cone; 5. Kop; 7. Mike Channon; 8. Us; 10. Lamp; 13. It; 14. Ian; 15. Reason; 19. Keel; 20. Alloa; 21. St; 23. Leyton; 24. An; 27. Sun; 28. Or; 29. Camel; 31. Mill; 35. On; 36. Oh.
Jumbled Name: PHIL THOMPSON.

Thank heavens I've scored! Sheffield Wednesday's Rodger Wylde is congratulated by happy team-mates after a vital 1976-77 League Cup goal against Wolves.

32

When the story broke that Rangers were interested in Hibs' brilliant midfield star Iain Munro the player was at a football game – at Ibrox!

"It's true," says the cultured player. "I was injured at the time and wasn't playing for Hibs. I got in contact with my former St. Mirren team-mate Bobby McKean, who had signed for Rangers the previous season, and asked him if he had any tickets for their forthcoming game, which was against Hearts in the League at Ibrox.

"Bobby left me a couple of tickets so I hobbled along to watch him play as Rangers won 3–1. Little did I know that I, too, would be a Rangers' player that same season!

"Anyway, I found out about all the speculation via the Sunday

delighted to find it was Rangers who had come in for me."

Munro joined Rangers in the swap deal for strikers Ally Scott and Graham Fyfe. One man who thought Rangers had got themselves a good player was – Celtic manager Jock Stein!

Stein had often admired the footwork, industry and enthusiasm of the versatile Munro, a naturally left-sided player.

Now Munro is putting his special skills on display at Ibrox where he has many clashes with his Old Firm pal Johnny Doyle, who joined Celtic almost at the same time he joined Rangers.

Both Doyle and Munro come from Uddingston, on the outskirts of Glasgow, and have retained a great friendship . . . although it is never

'SPECTATOR' RANGERS SIGNED

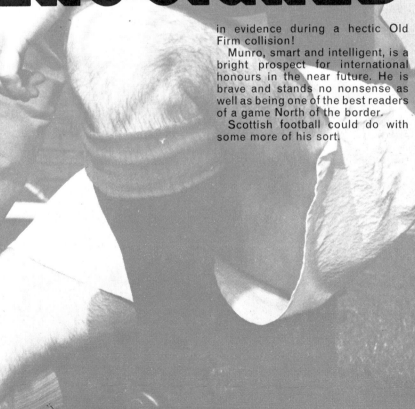

newspapers and, naturally, I was interested.

"There was also a whisper that Aberdeen might be interested with me going to Pittodrie and their midfield man Dave Robb going to join his former Dons' boss Eddie Turnbull at Easter Road.

"Obviously I preferred Ibrox and that is no slight against the Aberdeen boys. You see, it became fairly common knowledge that I had been a bit of a Rangers' fan in my youth.

"In fact, I started off as a Motherwell fan, but they kept selling their best players so I decided to move on myself and take my support elsewhere . . . and I took it to Ibrox.

"It was tremendous watching them. Jim Baxter was playing at left-half and I used to marvel at his skill and talent.

"And at outside-right was the amazing Willie Henderson, one of the greatest entertainers Scottish soccer has ever produced. That was a great Rangers side, but, naturally I like to think the present one is every bit as good.

"Anyway, when I finally left school I went to St. Mirren and from there to Hibs. I didn't really settle at Easter Road. I was played at fullback and in midfield and this didn't help me.

"Eventually I got the chance to move and, like I said earlier, I was

in evidence during a hectic Old Firm collision!

Munro, smart and intelligent, is a bright prospect for international honours in the near future. He is brave and stands no nonsense as well as being one of the best readers of a game North of the border.

Scottish football could do with some more of his sort.

NICK HOLMES Southampton

It's all happening for Ray Wilkins. Appointed captain of Chelsea at the age of 18, he has helped the Stamford Bridge club out of trouble and in 1976 won the first of his undoubtedly many England caps. Ray's good looks have also made him a favourite with the girls — but they also have two other Wilkins to follow! Ray's brothers, Graham and Steve, are professionals with Chelsea, too.

1846	The first soccer rules were written at Cambridge University.
1855	Sheffield, the oldest football club, formed.
1862	Notts County (the oldest League club) formed.
1863	On Monday, October 26th, The Football Association was formed. The meeting taking place at Freemasons Tavern, Great Queen Street, London.
1867	Queen's Park, the oldest Scottish club, formed.
1871	F.A. Cup introduced.
1872	Scotland, represented by the whole of the Queen's Park club, drew 0–0 with England at Hampden in the first official international match.
1872	Size of ball fixed.
1873	Scottish Football Association formed and Scottish Cup started.
1874	Sam Widdowson of Nottingham Forest introduced and registered shinguards.
1875	Crossbar first used instead of tape.
1876	Football Association of Wales formed.
1877	Football Association of Wales Challenge Cup introduced.
1878	First floodlight match, at Sheffield.
1878	Whistle used by referee for first time.
1880	Irish Football Association formed and Irish Cup introduced.
1882	International Board formed by four Home countries.
1882	Two-handed throw introduced.
1885	Professionalism legalised.
1885	Arbroath beat Bon Accord 36–0, a record for the Scottish Cup and the highest score in an official match in Great Britain.
1886	Caps awarded for the first time for international matches.
1887	Preston beat Hyde 26–0 in the F.A. Cup, still a record for a match in England.
1888	The Football League founded by Mr. W. McGregor.
1889	Preston North End are the first team to perform the Double. They won the Championship without losing a match and won the F.A. Cup without conceding a goal.
1890	Irish League formed.
1890	Goalnets used for first time.
1891	Scottish League formed.
1891	Penalty-kick introduced at request of the Irish F.A.
1891	Referee and linesmen used instead of umpires.
1892	Second Division of the Football League formed.
1892	Goal-nets used for first time in an F.A. Cup Final (W.B.A. and Aston Villa).

1893	First F.A. Amatuer Cup.
1894	Southern League formed.
1895	F.A. Cup stolen from a shop window in Birmingham and never recovered.
1897	Aston Villa became the second team to win the F.A. Cup and League Championship double.
1898	Glasgow Rangers won every game played by them in Scottish First Division.
1899	Promotion and Relegation introduced end of 1898-99 season.
1902	The Ibrox Park disaster, in which 25 people died when terracing collapsed.
1903	Bury beat Derby County 6–0 in F.A. Cup Final – still a record.
1904	F.I.F.A. formed in Paris.
1905	Goalkeepers ordered to stay on goal-line for penalty kicks.
1905	The first £1,000 transfer when Alf Common is transferred from Sunderland to Middlesbrough.
1907	Players Union, now known as the P.F.A.. is revived,
1908	F.A. Charity Shield introduced.
1912	Goalkeepers' use of hands

ABOVE . . . The famous 'White Horse' Final between Bolton and West Ham in 1923.

BELOW . . . The shop from which the original F.A. Cup was stolen. A reward brought no result.

BELOW . . . The 1914 F.A. Cup Final between Burnley and Liverpool, at Crystal Palace. George V attended the match.
ABOVE, RIGHT . . . Dixie Dean, record-breaking Everton striker.

ABOVE . . . Crowds swarm over the walls at the first F.A. Cup Final at Wembley in 1923.

BELOW . . . Italy manager Vittorio Pozzo holds the 1938 World Cup after his team had beaten Hungary 4–2 in the Final.

BELOW . . . Arsenal's Ted Drake once scored seven goals from eight shots against Aston Villa.

	restricted to penalty-area.
1913	Distance extended from six to ten yards for opponents at free-kicks.
1914	King George V the first reigning monarch to attend a F.A. Cup Final – Burnley and Liverpool at the Crystal Palace.
1919	Football League extended to 44 clubs, 22 in each of the First and Second Divisions.
1920	Third Division South formed with 22 clubs.
1921	Third Division North formed with 20 clubs. (In 1923 two extra teams, Doncaster Rovers and New Brighton, made it 22).
1921	Goalkeepers in International games had to wear deep yellow jerseys.
1923	Bolton Wanderers beat West Ham in the first-ever Wembley F.A. Cup Final.
1924	First international at Wembley when England played Scotland.
1925	Offside rule altered from three to two defenders between attacker and goal.
1926	Huddersfield Town first team to complete hat-trick of League

	Championships.
1927	Cardiff City beat Arsenal 1–0 in the F.A. Cup Final and so became the first team to take the Cup out of England.
1927	First radio commentary on an F.A. Cup Final.
1928	Britain left F.I.F.A. owing to a dispute over the definition of amateurism and 'broken time' payments for amateurs.
1928	David Jack joins Arsenal from Bolton Wanderers for £10,340 – the first ever £10,000 transfer.
1928	Dixie Dean of Everton scores 60 goals in the First Division for a new League record. Dean also scored 22 goals in other games.
1929	England lost their first international on foreign soil when Spain won 4–3 in Madrid.
1929	Goalkeepers ordered to stand still on goal-line until penalty-kick is taken.
1930	Brentford became first Football League club to win all 21 home matches.
1930	World Cup started and Uruguay beat Argentina 4–2 in Final to become the first holders.
1931	West Bromwich Albion became the first team to win the F.A. Cup and promotion from the Second Division.
1933	Everton hat-trick, winning the Second Division Championship, First Division title and F.A. Cup in successive seasons.
1934	Italy beat Czechoslovakia 2–1 after extra-time in the second World Cup Final.
1935	Arsenal equal Huddersfield Town feat of winning the First Division Championship three seasons in succession.
1935	Arsenal's Ted Drake scored seven goals at Aston Villa, a record for an away game in the First Division.
1935	Official two-referee trials.
1936	Luton Town beat Bristol Rovers 12–0 with Joe Payne scoring 10 – still a record for a Football League match.
1936	Charlton Athletic win promotion from the Second Division, thus becoming the first team to go from the Third to First Division in two seasons.
1936	Dixie Dean passed Steve Bloomers' aggregate League scoring record of 352. Dean finally finished with 379.
1937	British record of 149,547 watch Scotland and England play at Hampden Park.
1938	Italy beat Hungary 4–2 in the third World Cup Final.
1938	F.A.'s 75th anniversary.
1938	Laws of the Game rewritten.

CONTINUED ON PAGE 40

LIAM BRADY
Arsenal and
Republic
of Ireland

38

BRIAN HORTON
Brighton

CONTINUED FROM PAGE 37

1939	Numbering of players made compulsory in League matches.
1946	Great Britain rejoined F.I.F.A.
1946	Disaster at Burnden Park, Bolton, when 33 were killed and over 400 injured when crash barriers collapsed in Cup-tie against Stoke City.
1947	Doncaster set up new record with 72 points in Third Division (North).
1948	Frank Swift becomes the first goalkeeper to captain England – against Italy in Turin.
1948	Record for British club match, apart from Cup Finals, when 143,570 watch Rangers play Hibernian at Hampden Park.
1948	Record attendance for an English League match when 82,950 watch Manchester United play Arsenal at Maine Road.
1949	Glasgow Rangers become first Scottish club to win League, Cup and League Cup in same season.
1950	Football League extended from 88 to 92 clubs.
1950	Uruguay win the fourth World Cup when they beat Brazil.
1950	Scotland first beaten at home by foreign side when Austria win 1–0 at Hampden Park.
1950	Jimmy Mullen (Wolves) becomes England's first-ever substitute when he replaced Jackie Milburn v Belgium in Brussels.
1951	Use of white ball legalised.
1953	Derek Dooley, Sheffield Wednesday's centre-forward, had a leg amputated after being injured in a League game v Preston.
1953	Arsenal won the League Championship for a record seventh time.
1953	F.A.'s 90th anniversary.
1953	Hungary inflict England's first ever defeat on their own soil when they win 6–3 at Wembley.
1954	England have their biggest ever international defeat when Hungary win 7–1 in Budapest.
1954	West Germany beat Hungary 4–2 in the Final to win the fifth World Cup.
1955	The first European Cup games are played.
1955	Floodlighting used for the first time in an international match when they are switched on for the England v Spain match at Wembley.
1955	Denis Wilshaw becomes the first English player to score four goals against Scotland as England win 7–2 at Wembley.
1956	Floodlights are used for the first time in a Football League match when Portsmouth played Newcastle at Fratton Park.
1957	Entertainment Tax withdrawn.

1958	The Munich air crash, eight Manchester United players are killed.
1958	Brazil beat Sweden 5–2 in the sixth World Cup Final.
1958	Divisions Three and Four replaced the Third South and North.
1961	England beat Scotland 9–3 at Wembley.
1961	Tottenham Hotspur become the first team this century to win the League and F.A. Cup Double.
1961	Peterborough United, in their first season of League football, win the Fourth Division Championship and score 134 goals, an all-time League record.
1962	Manchester United become the first English side to pay over £100,000 transfer fee when they sign Denis Law from Turin.

ABOVE . . . Hungary celebrate their 6–3 victory over England in November, 1953.
LEFT . . . Hungary's second goal in that memorable match at Wembley.

Spurs' skipper Danny Blanchflower after their Double triumph.

ABOVE . . . Jimmy Greaves scores during England's 9–3 defeat of Scotland.
BELOW . . . England have that World Cup-winning feeling!

BELOW . . . Tommy Gemmell's goal puts Celtic on the way to winning the 1967 European Cup Final against Inter Milan.

RIGHT . . . Manchester United kept the European Cup in Britain with a breathtaking display against Benfica at Wembley in 1968.

BELOW . . . Rangers parade their "grand slam" of trophies in 1975–76.
BOTTOM . . . Stoke City with the 1972 League Cup.

1962	Brazil beat Czechoslovakia 3–1 to win the seventh World Cup Final.
1963	F.A. Centenary and Football League's 75th Jubilee.
1963	English "retain and transfer" system ruled illegal in High Court test case.
1964	Over 300 people killed and 500 injured in World's worst-ever disaster. It happened in Peru, when rioting broke out in an Olympic Games qualifying match against Argentina.
1965	Arthur Rowley retired after setting new all-time League record of 434 League goals.
1966	Substitutes allowed in League games.
1966	England beat West Germany 4–2

	after extra-time at Wembley to win eighth World Cup Final.
1967	Manchester United win the League Championship for the seventh time, to equal the record of Arsenal and Liverpool.
1967	Glasgow Celtic become the first British side to win the European Cup.
1968	Manchester United become the first English side to win the European Cup, beating Benfica 4–1 after extra-time.
1970	Martin Peters becomes the first player to be involved in a £200,000 transfer, Peters joined Tottenham from West Ham and Jimmy Greaves was transferred to West Ham in the deal.
1970	Brazil beat Italy 4–1 in the Final to win the ninth World Cup.
1971	The second Ibrox Park disaster when 66 people are crushed to death near the end of the Rangers v Celtic match.
1971	Arsenal become the fourth team to perform the League and F.A. Cup Double.
1971	Arsenal pay £200,000 to Everton for Alan Ball.
1972	Stoke City win their first major trophy in 109 years by beating Chelsea 2–1 in the Final of the Football League Cup.
1972	Hereford United, after some great F.A. Cup feats, are elected to the Football League at the expense of Barrow.
1973	The Football League decide that a 'three-up-and-three-down' promotion and relegation system between the top three Divisions will operate in the Football League.
1973	Ted Croker is the new secretary of the Football Association.
1974	Sir Alf Ramsey, who was manager when England won the 1966 World Cup is sacked by the F.A. and is replaced as England manager by Don Revie.
1974	West Germany beat Holland 2–1 in the Final of the tenth World Cup.
1974	Martin Dobson joins Everton from Burnley in the first £300,000 cash transfer.
1975	Scottish League football is reformed into three Divisions. Ten clubs in the new Premier and 14 clubs in each of the First and Second Division.
1976	Goal difference replaced goal average in the Football League for the start of the 1976–77 season.
1976	Football League referee rule change. In future they will use yellow cards for booking players and red cards for sending off offences. Rangers do the grand slam of trophies in Scotland.

41

JOE SMITH
Aberdeen

42

Two stars of the Midlands . . . Birmingham City winger Gary Jones (above) and Tony Brown, the West Bromwich Albion goal-poacher.

LEFT . . . Steve Perryman of Spurs stops the progress of Trevor Whymark, the Ipswich Town striker.
RIGHT . . . Colin Todd, the Derby County defender, finds himself leg-locked during a game against West Brom.
BELOW . . . The tackle from Phil Neal of Liverpool sends Leeds' Peter Lorimer sprawling, but the referee said "no penalty".

ONE AGAINST ONE

LEFT . . . The speed of Norwich City winger Jimmy Neighbour is too much for Middlesbrough's Stuart Boam on this occasion.
RIGHT . . . Stoke City's Terry Conroy (stripes) gets in his shot before Q.P.R.'s Dave Webb can tackle.

ABOVE . . . Bristol City captain Geoff Merrick gets up higher than his Arsenal challenger.

45

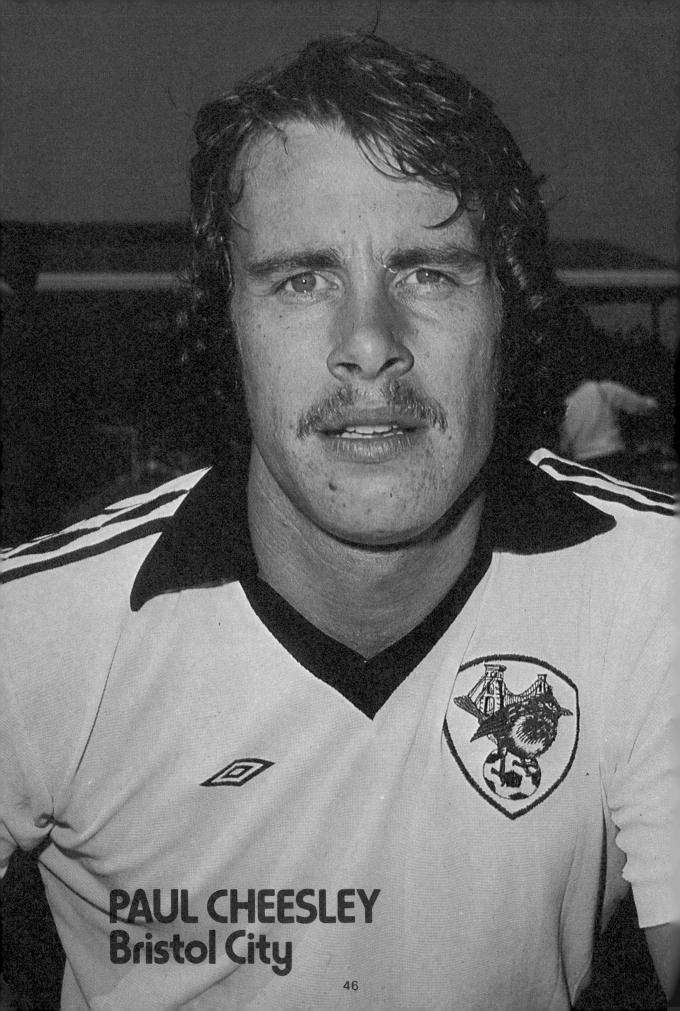

PAUL CHEESLEY
Bristol City

46

PROUD father . . . Lincoln City goal-keeper Peter Grotier with his four-year-old twin sons Dean (left) and Paul.

47

The moment Jeff Blockley will never forget

The F.A. Cup has a habit of making players heroes overnight. "Unknowns" suddenly become the talking point of soccer because of their sensational feats.

But this didn't happen to Leicester City captain Jeff Blockley. He has a bitter memory of the famous competition.

In one moment of uncertainty, his whole career suddenly took a turn for the worse and it needed time and a transfer to get over it.

The moment was during the Semi-Final of the F.A. Cup at Hillsborough, 1973.

Blockley, as Arsenal centre-half, in the first-half tried to pass the ball back to goalkeeper Bob Wilson.

Nine times out of ten there would have been no problem, but he recalls: "I saw Bob coming off his line. I didn't want to lob the ball over him. In the end, I didn't put enough power into my pass and Vic Halom had the easiest of chances to score."

Sunderland went on to win the F.A. Cup Final against Leeds – "no consolation to me" – but from that moment, Blockley was out of favour with the Arsenal fans.

"I felt dreadful after the game," he says. "These things happen in soccer, though . . . you've just got to get over them."

The Gunners' supporters wouldn't forget it, though, and in the end a transfer was the only solution.

"Although my two years at Highbury were not exactly successful, I wouldn't have missed them for anything.

"They are such a big club and the experience of being with them is unforgettable.

"I made the mistake of being inhibited . . . overawed. I'm naturally a talker, yet at Highbury I tended to stay quiet.

"I learnt a lot there and I reckon I left Arsenal a better professional than when I arrived."

Blockley left Highbury in the winter of 1974–75 for Leicester, who snapped him up for half the £200,000 Arsenal had paid Coventry City.

The move worked wonders. Blockley allowed his true personality to "show through" again and proved that he is a much better player than most Arsenal fans gave him credit for.

Blockley was, in fact, born in Leicester and admits that he had "no hesitation" in signing for them when they came in for him.

The centre-half soon established

what must surely be a record – he tore a cartilage in two successive games!

He was injured in the last match of 1974–75 – and in the opening game of 1975–76. Both injuries needed a cartilage operation!

Blockley's presence at the heart of Leicester's defence has certainly made them much stronger, adding steel to the skill that has always been associated with Filbert Street.

"I don't play any fancy stuff," he says. "I'm aggressive and go out to win the ball. Every team needs someone like this.

"Being appointed captain was marvellous . . . gave me a real boost. I've always been a shouter on the field and now I can encourage the lads all the time."

It was more than a coincidence that Leicester's form improved dramatically when Blockley arrived at Filbert Street.

They narrowly missed out on a U.E.F.A. Cup place in 1976, but the future for City is certainly bright.

Excitement from the F.A. Cup . . . John Mitchell of Fulham is beaten by the combined effort of Swindon Town defender John Trollope and goalkeeper Jimmy Allen.

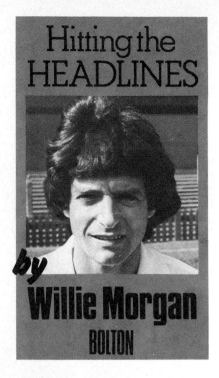

Hitting the HEADLINES

by **Willie Morgan**
BOLTON

Burnley before my transfer to Manchester United in August, 1968," remembers Morgan fondly.

"One particular game that sticks out above all the others occurred in a First Division clash against, funnily enough, Manchester United at Turf Moor.

"It was Christmas, 1964, and we took United to the cleaners and thrashed them 6–1. From a personal point of view, I remember the match because I actually scored a couple of goals. And for someone who is not renowned to be a goalscorer that was quite a feat."

Morgan's superb form that day must have left a deep impression on the then Old Trafford boss, Matt Busby, because Morgan made headlines again when Busby returned to Turf Moor and signed the Burnley winger for £100,000.

"My performance that day against United might have helped," he says. "But Mr. Busby was certainly forced into the transfer market when regular winger John Aston broke a leg. And as I had asked for a

"Like when I played against Estudiantes in the World Club Championship," says Morgan. "Even though we lost 2–1 on aggregate – I scored our goal – it was a real experience.

"Another proud moment for me at Old Trafford was when I was appointed captain."

But then things turned sour for the Glasgow-born star when he fell out of favour with manager Tommy Docherty and was eventually sold back to his former club Burnley.

"Without going into details about the rift at Old Trafford, I can assure you I felt very low at the time," explains Willie.

His return to Turf Moor didn't last very long before he was on the move again. This time to Bolton Wanderers.

"In a way I regretted returning to Turf Moor because of the travelling involved. You see, I lived in Altrincham, Cheshire, and the journey each day really got me down."

But a move nearer home was always on the cards and it came as

'I helped thrash Man. United 6—1'

During his career with Burnley (twice), Manchester United and Bolton Wanderers, Willie Morgan has had his share of the headlines. Some of it good, some bad, but has the likeable winger ever let it affect him?

"You can't," says Morgan. "If you do it could ruin your career. I don't mind criticism, but I'll only ever listen to my manager. After all, he selects the side each week."

Morgan seems to have been playing in League football a long time. Can he remember when he first hit the headlines?

"I suppose it was when I made my first-team debut," recalls Morgan, "for Burnley against Sheffield Wednesday at Hillsborough in April, 1963.

"I was just 18 when selected for the important clash with Wednesday. Burnley were making a determined bid for the First Division Championship and the Sheffield club were not far behind.

"I started my League career in the best possible way – with a 1–0 victory."

Although Morgan made only one other appearance during 1962–63 Burnley did well to finish third, a point behind Spurs and seven adrift of Champions Everton.

But Willie didn't take long to become a regular and he went on to make over 200 appearances for the club.

"I had many happy times at

transfer, he bought me."

Morgan certainly had his ups and downs at Old Trafford.

no real shock when he did move to Burnden Park although, as ever, it did make the national Press.

Willie scores against Estudiantes in the infamous 1968 World Cup Championship.

Hitting the HEADLINES

by Bryan Robson
WEST HAM

Robson really hit the headlines during the 1968–69 season when he scored 21 League goals and helped Newcastle United win the Fairs Cup (now U.E.F.A. Cup).

"The season before our run in Europe, we finished a lowly 10th in the First Division," says Robson. "And through the 'one club, one city' rule that applied then we somehow qualified."

Despite the controversy that raged with the ruling, Newcastle were determined to make the most of their chance in Europe.

"The atmosphere within the club was fantastic," recalls Pop. "The supporters were out of this world, behind us all the way."

They certainly were. Their lowest gate for the entire run was in the First Round when 46,300 turned up for the clash with Feyenoord!

"We were a little nervous, but once we settled down and found our rhythm we beat the Dutch aces 4–0. It was a good start for us."

In the return, Newcastle progressed through but not without some anxious moments. The Rotterdamers fought hard but could only pull two back.

"The next game, against Sporting Lisbon, was a very tight match," he says. "We had to travel to Lisbon for the first-leg and did tremendously well to hold them to a 1–1 draw."

In front of 53,650 fans it needed a vintage goal from Robson to settle the tie and put United into Round Three.

"I enjoyed scoring that goal, and the noise that greeted it was incredible," remembers Robson.

Round Three proved to be their toughest game. Their opponents Real Zaragoza had won 3–2 in the first-leg in Spain. It was those two away goals that were so vital in the return at St. James' Park where Newcastle scraped home 2–1, to go through on the away goals counting double rule.

"Those two games were very tense affairs indeed," says Robson. "Over the two legs, I scored probably two of my best goals. The first one in Spain resulted from a cross that Wyn Davies nodded down to me and I volleyed the ball home.

"The second goal, at home, was a very important one. It was imperative we scored early, and it came after just a couple of minutes.

"I collected a pass and from about 30 yards hammered in an unstoppable shot which nearly brought St. James' Park down."

Newcastle went on to the Semi-Finals when they eliminated Vitoria Setubal 6–4 on aggregate in the Quarter-Finals with Pop scoring another two.

The Magpies were then paired with Glasgow Rangers in the Semis and got a tremendous 0–0 draw at Ibrox. In front of a 60,000 crowd,

'Two great goals — in two legs'

Joe Harvey's lads won a Final place with a 2–0 victory.

Newcastle had home advantage in the first-leg of the Final against Ujpest Dozsa and built up a commanding 3–0 lead to take to Hungary.

The return was very tense, particularly after Dozsa had pulled back two goals, but Newcastle weren't to be denied and scored three to capture the Fairs Cup for the first time in the club's history on a 6–2 aggregate.

Robson says: "Of the two games, I think the first-leg was the most important because we knew we had to build up a big lead and three was enough.

"The reception and scenes that greeted our homecoming were too incredible to describe."

Newcastle United v. Ujpest Dozsa in the 1969 Fairs Cup Final.

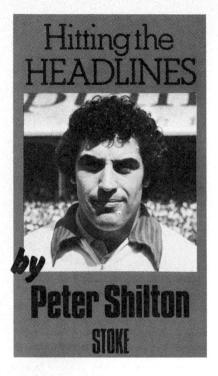

Hitting the HEADLINES

by Peter Shilton

STOKE

Peter Shilton has grabbed the soccer headlines on many occasions since he burst into the Leicester City first-team at the ripe old age of 16.

That was during the 1966–67 season when he made four appearances and he performed admirably. Because of the up-and-coming Shilton, Leicester were able to sell their England number one Gordon Banks to Stoke City. A path that Peter was to follow after Gordon's motor accident.

"When I first broke into the Leicester League side, Gordon was on England duty," says Peter. "And I wasn't in the least overawed by the fact I was stepping into the shoes of England's number one 'keeper."

Continues Shilton: "I was just intent on giving a good performance and not letting the manager or my team-mates down."

He certainly didn't disgrace anyone. City were in the enviable position of having two top-class goalkeepers. Surely, the club couldn't keep them both happy?

"I thought I would go and I was determined to leave. But the club obviously realised they could get a bigger fee for Gordon than me."

In March, 1967, Stoke City boss Tony Waddington took Banks from Filbert Street for around £50,000. And Peter became the first-team 'keeper.

Did Gordon have any real influence on the career of Shilton?

"No, not really," recalls the Leicester-born 'keeper. "We had the normal relationship you would expect with first and reserve-team goalkeepers.

"Gordon was a very professional player. But I did not model myself on him. The one person who had a big influence on my career was George Dewis.

"He had coached me since I first arrived at Filbert Street at the age of 11.

"George is the 'A' team coach and has been at the club for over 30 years. Yes, he was a big help in my early days."

In 1969, Shilton played a big part in helping Leicester reach the Final of the F.A. Cup against Manchester City at Wembley – despite being relegated to the Second Division that same season.

"Going down was a big disappointment for everyone at the club," remembers Shilton. "But we had some compensation when we reached Wembley Stadium.

"In the League, our luck seemed to desert us. Games we deserved to win or draw, we were losing by the odd goal.

"In the Cup, though, it was a different story. We won every game up to the Final by a single goal margin – we certainly had the luck with us in our Cup run.

"As for The Final I thought we were very unlucky against Manchester City. We could so easily have won the Cup, for the first time in the club's history, but were beaten by a Neil Young goal."

Shilton helped Leicester back to the First Division in 1970–71, and then in November, 1974, a massive £325,000 was paid to City from Stoke for the services of the Eng and goalkeeper – a path Banks had taken over seven years previously.

"It was pure coincidence that I followed Gordon. He had been badly injured in a car accident and Stoke had tried out two other 'keepers, John Farmer and Mike McDonald, before they came for me. My club paid out a record fee for a 'keeper."

Although Shilton was transferred under unfortunate circumstances one thing is certain – he would have fetched that massive fee from any of the top clubs.

'My Club paid a record fee for me'

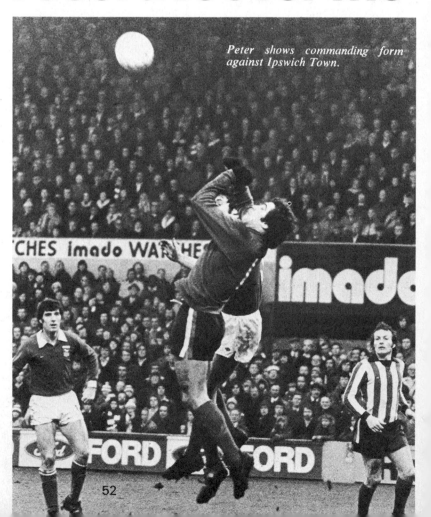

Peter shows commanding form against Ipswich Town.

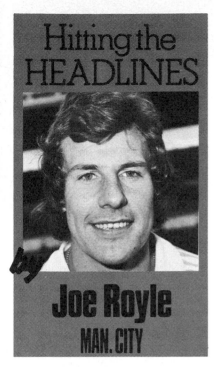

Hitting the HEADLINES

by Joe Royle
MAN. CITY

During Everton's march to the 1969–70 Football League Championship, Joe Royle emerged as an exciting prospect. And in that campaign certainly fulfilled his potential and blossomed into one of the best centre-forwards in the First Division.

"I was fortunate to have an injury-free season," remembers Royle. "I appeared in all 42 League games during our title run.

"The atmosphere in the club was fantastic. Everton had done very well the season before when we finished third and were naturally confident of the forthcoming term."

The club certainly had plenty of reasons to feel optimistic about the 1969–70 season.

Recalls the big number nine: "Manager at the time, Harry Catterick, had assembled a very strong first-team squad. When you see a list of players like Gordon West, Tommy Wright, Brian Labone, Keith Newton, Alan Ball, Howard Kendall and Jimmy Husband, you can understand why we were so confident."

The Toffees started the campaign in true Championship style, spearheaded by Joe Royle.

"We won the first six or seven games on the trot," says Royle. "That was when we realised if we could maintain that sort of consistency we would be there or thereabouts when the Championship was decided."

But it wasn't roses all the way, as Joe remembers:

"Just after Christmas we went slightly off the boil and dropped a few silly points. But we soon got over that patch and began winning again."

In the end Everton powered to the League title with a stunning number of 66 points.

"That was a disappointment in a way," says the Liverpool-born striker, "because we finished just one point adrift of the then-record number of points held by Leeds.

"But we consoled ourselves with the fact we finished nine points clear of the runners-up – Leeds."

But what of Royle's contribution to the team's efforts? How did he feel the campaign went for him?

"I was very pleased, personally," he says. "I scored 23 League goals. It was my highest tally since I broke into the first-team as a 16-year-old in 1966."

Among those 23 goals, which did he think was the most important?

"Every single one," says Royle: "They all counted at the end of that season. If I must choose one, though, I would plump for the winner I scored against Coventry City at Highfield Road.

"We were being out-played and hanging on for a point with the score 0–0. Jimmy Husband received the ball wide on the right, he cut inside, crossed the ball, and I was running in on my own to hit the ball home with only a few minutes remaining.

"That was two valuable away points and we really believed we could win the title."

Joe Royle is still scoring goals, only now it's with Manchester City after his headline-making £200,000 transfer from Goodison Park in March, 1975.

'SCORING 23 GOALS IN EVERTON'S CHAMPIONSHIP SEASON'

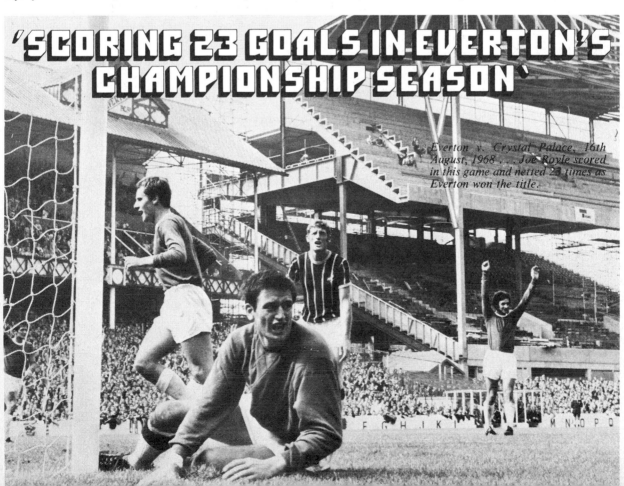

Everton v. Crystal Palace, 16th August, 1968 ... Joe Royle scored in this game and netted 23 times as Everton won the title.

The DERBY COUNTY story

WEMBLEY WIN LIFTS GYPSY'S CURSE

When Dave Mackay played his last game for Derby County against West Brom at the Baseball Ground on 1st May, 1971, his boss at the time Brian Clough, said: "I hope Dave never becomes a manager. He's been too busy being a great player to learn all sides of the game."

Well, Dave did become a manager: of Swindon, Nottingham Forest and then in October, 1973, of Derby County when Clough and his assistant Peter Taylor left after a series of disagreements.

Said Clough when he heard Mackay was replacing him: "I feel sorry for him. It will take him three years to undo what we did at the Baseball Ground."

Mackay's reign, in fact, lasted three years, one month and two days!

But bringing the ageless warrior to the Baseball Ground in the first place as a player was a masterstroke by Clough. But then so was Derby's decision to persuade Clough and his assistant Peter Taylor to leave Hartlepool and join them in June, 1967.

Together, Clough, Taylor and Mackay brought First Division football back to a club that had drifted to near obscurity . . . a club barely able to survive in the Second . . . a club that appeared to go from one crisis to another.

Today, Derby County are established as one of the top sides in Europe, a team respected wherever they play.

They began in 1884 as part of Derbyshire County Cricket Club and four years later became one of the 12 founder members of the Football League.

Derby County F.C. kicked-off their League career with a 6–3 win over Bolton Wanderers, and went on to finish 10th in the table.

In 1895 they moved from their ground at Nottingham Road to the Baseball Ground, so named because it was used by troops for playing baseball.

A soccer legend has it that

ABOVE . . . Steve Bloomer scored 28 goals in 24 appearances for England and 291 during his Derby career.
RIGHT . . . Raich Carter, one of the finest inside-forwards ever seen.

gypsies were thrown off the ground to make room for the footballers and were so angry laid a curse against the club winning an honour in the game.

Whether you believe in such superstitions or not, it certainly seemed that Fate did not shine too brightly on Derby County in the early years.

The League Championship eluded them, so did the F.A. Cup. In fact, in 1903 Derby were on the receiving end of Bury's 6–0 win, still the biggest F.A. Cup Final victory to this day.

Their first success came 43 years later, in 1946, when they beat Charlton 4–1 to win the trophy at Wembley.

A few days before the Final, though, captain and full-back Jack Nicholas crossed some gypsy palms with silver – as a precaution.

Mind you, a few thousand Derby hearts sank when the Final went into extra-time.

Before their Wembley triumph, Derby had shuttled between the First and Second Divisions several times, until 1926 when a settled period of relative success kept them in the top grade until 1953.

Into that era had come some great County stars. Men such as Steve Bloomer, who played continuously from 1892 to 1914.

Bloomer scored 28 goals in 24 games for England and 291 in his career with County. He also hit 61 in six years with Middlesbrough.

But after just five matches in the 1913–14 season he retired – and Derby slipped into Division Two.

After Bloomer came winger Sammy Crooks, who arrived from Durham with his boots wrapped in a brownpaper parcel. He went on to make 408 League appearances for

County and win 26 caps for England.

Two other England stars were centre-half Jack Barker and centre-forward Jack Bowers, who in 1930–31 scored 37 League goals, a club record he shares with Ray Straw.

Then there was Harry Storer, later to manage the club, and Scottish international "Dally" Duncan – so named because of his childhood habit of walking slowly behind his father and kicking stones.

Duncan, at 37, was still on Derby's wing for the 1946 Cup Final, a match that really belonged to a couple of the finest inside-forwards the world has ever seen – Raich Carter of England and Northern Ireland's Peter Doherty.

Another hero at Wembley was Jack Stamps, the scorer of two of his side's four goals.

But players grow older and fairly soon after the club's first major honour, the team dismantled.

Derby remained in the First Division, though, and gates actually went up, attracted by the skills of Johnny Morris and Billy Steel, big money signings from Manchester United and Morton.

But no attention was given to rebuilding for the future. No new talent was waiting for the chance to replace old stars and the worst fears were realised in 1953 when Derby were relegated.

Two seasons later they slid even further down the soccer scale – into the Third.

They were good enough to take

ABOVE . . . 1946 F.A. Cup Final action from Wembley. Derby beat Charlton 4–1, The Rams' first success in the Cup.

ABOVE . . . 1946 F.A. Cup Final action from Wembley. Derby beat Charlton 4–1, The Rams' first success in the Cup.

BELOW . . . Derby County pose for the cameramen before the beginning of the 1976/77 season.

one step back in 1955–56 when they won promotion with Grimsby Town.

Manager at the time was Harry Storer, their ex-player brought from Coventry in a desperate effort to restore the club's pride and prestige.

Under Storer's leadership, Derby survived in the Second Division, but with the emphasis on the physical side of the game rather than skill. The First Division still seemed a long, long way off.

Eventually Storer was sacked and Tim Ward, the former Barnsley, Grimsby and Carlisle manager took over.

But after several boardroom disputes, Ward resigned, saying: "Every time I wanted to buy a player

they told me I couldn't go above the £10,000 I paid Swansea for Eddie Thomas. I couldn't even post a letter without boardroom approval."

But two players Ward did sign went on to become top stars and help the club to glory. They were Kevin Hector from Bradford P.A. and Alan Durban from Cardiff.

So Tim Ward departed and in June, 1967, after Derby had ended the season in 17th place in Division Two, Brian Clough and Peter Taylor were appointed.

Clough realised the team needed rebuilding and somehow got the money the directors refused Tim Ward.

Striker John O'Hare was brought

from Sunderland for £23,000. Next came centre-half Roy McFarland from Tranmere for a similar fee.

Clough was rebuilding, but he needed a corner-stone. That rock came in the shape of Dave Mackay, who at the time was considering leaving Spurs to return to his former club Hearts as player-manager.

Then came midfielder Willie Carlin from Sheffield United to complete Phase One of Clough's plans.

The new-look Derby was obviously too good for the Second Division and at the end of the 1968–69 season were promoted along with runners-up Crystal Palace.

Back in the First, Clough hadn't finished spending. On February 6th, 1970 he signed Terry Hennessey from Nottingham Forest for £110,000 – the club's first six-figure fee.

Derby ended their first season back in the top grade fourth in the table to earn a place in Europe . . . in the old Fairs Cup.

But the club didn't compete. They were found guilty of "gross negligence in administration" and banned from Europe for a year.

The whole of Derby were stunned and directors resigned. But Brian Clough signed a new contract and went out to spend £65,000 on Archie Gemmill (from Preston) and

£170,000 on Colin Todd (from Sunderland). He was determined to take the club to the very top.

In 1971 Dave Mackay played his final game for Derby and went off to take over Swindon Town.

A year later, in 1971–72, Derby County were acclaimed Champions for the first time in their history when they finished on 58 points, one ahead of Leeds and Liverpool. The gypsy's curse had well and truly been laid . . . or had it?

On 15th October, 1973, after several disputes behind-the-scenes, Brian Clough and Peter Taylor resigned.

This action was the result of a letter from chairman Mr. Sam Longson ordering Clough to cease writing for newspapers and appearing on TV.

Fans demonstrated for his reinstatement. Players demanded his return, but chairman Longson refused.

On October 23rd, the Derby drama continued when Dave Mackay was announced as the new manager. Immediately the players threatened strike action.

Four days later, however, Derby drew 0–0 at West Ham and Mackay told waiting Pressmen: "I'm de-

ABOVE . . . Brian Clough and Peter Taylor with the Championship, May, 1974.

LEFT . . . Derby beat Real Madrid 3–0 in the European Cup at the Baseball Ground, but lost 5–1 in Spain.

lighted with our performance today and the professional attitude of the players."

Finally, after a further outburst by the players and Clough's departure to Brighton, peace appeared to be restored at the Baseball Ground. There were still rumours. Players were still unhappy. Discipline perhaps was not what it should be.

Despite this hidden resentment in some quarters, Derby ended the 1973–74 term in third position.

The following season, Dave Mackay took The Rams to the title and into Europe again.

Even though Derby were a team of quality with Archie Gemmill, Roy McFarland, Bruce Rioch, Henry Newton, Francis Lee, David Nish, Rod Thomas, Roger Davies, Kevin Hector, Colin Todd and Colin Boulton, their attempts to win Europe's most coveted crown ended in failure.

After gaining a three goal lead against Real Madrid in the European Cup Second Round first-leg, they

were beaten 5–1 in the return in Spain to go out 6–5. A disastrous result for Derby and English football.

Star of Derby's tremendous first-leg game at the Baseball Ground

was Charlie George, brought from Arsenal for a bargain £100,000.

Mackay had tamed and utilised the superb skills of the player they labelled: "The Problem Boy of Highbury".

Despite that setback in Europe, Derby went on that 1975–76 season to reach the F.A. Cup Semi-Finals and end fourth. Derby's trouble wasn't scoring goals – but stopping them.

Manager Mackay entered 1976–77 with this resolve: "I shall never forsake our attacking policy. I have every confidence in Derby County and the future of the club."

Three months later Dave Mackay was denied a vote of confidence from the board, and left.

Derby surprisingly chose "unknown" Colin Murphy as their new boss . . . the man brought from Nottingham Forest by Mackay to look after the Central League side.

But another sensation was to rock Derby a few weeks later, when an attempt was made to persuade Brian Clough to return "home" to the Baseball Ground.

After two days of negotiations he rejected Derby's offer and said: "I have wanted this job every day since I left over three years ago. But I'm staying at Forest."

Nothing is certain in football except that Derby will continue to make dramatic headlines both on and off the field.

ABOVE . . . Derby versus Manchester United, August, 1976. Roy McFarland tackles Lou Macari.

LEFT . . . Dave Mackay was sacked during 1976/77 season.

BELOW . . . Colin Murphy was promoted to succeed Mackay.

"SOCCER ON TV IS A WINNER"

There's nothing I like better after a hard training session, or a tough match, than to sit down at home with my feet up in front of the telly.

My favourites are those American cops and robbers series such as Columbo, Kojak, Police Story and Starksy and Hutch. It's the ideal way to relax.

Put crime, violence or almost any other subject on TV, great! But mention soccer on the box and immediately the arguments start.

Is TV good or bad for the game? That's been the subject of so much controversy over the past few years.

The critics claim it keeps people in their armchairs, away from matches.

Leeds United manager Jimmy Armfield said in SHOOT last year that he firmly believes Saturday lunchtime football previews are partly to blame for fans' disenchantment with "live" soccer.

Mr. Armfield reckons features such as "On The Ball' and B.B.C.'s "Football Focus" show too many goals from the best matches.

The result is spectators go along to League games on Saturday afternoons expecting to see the same thing. When it doesn't happen they feel cheated and stop coming.

The Leeds boss added he'd like to see "Match of the Day" taken off and televised matches restricted to Sunday afternoons.

He made the point that some fans get to know which games are going to be televised and stay at home, content to watch the match on the box at night.

Mr. Armfield makes sense and puts forward a good case against, but personally I'm in favour of soccer on TV.

We've got to face facts. TV is now part of the game. Clubs have spent a fortune on improving their floodlights to make them suitable for colour TV.

Banning cameras from our League

This goal by Bobby Charlton ensured European Cup success for Manchester United against Benfica in 1968.

grounds would be a bad thing.

Soccer on the telly brings entertainment to many millions and doesn't keep the *real* fan away from games.

To them there's nothing like "live" action, being on the scene and part of the atmosphere. For them football on the box is a bonus.

But what about the people who can't get to matches on a Saturday?

The sick, the aged, the shopkeepers, men on certain shifts in factories or in public services, the tens of thousands who play the game and those who live many miles from the nearest League ground.

Why deprive them of watching the big games and watching the top stars?

Mind you, I wouldn't like to see *more* soccer on TV. I think the present coverage is about right.

Normally throughout a season there's a midweek Cup-tie or international, followed by B.B.C.'s "Match of the Day" on Saturday evenings and I.T.V.'s "The Big Match" or "Star Soccer" on Sunday afternoons.

One of the highlights of a Saturday for me is the soccer magazine programmes "On The Ball" with Brian Moore, or Bob Wilson's "Football Focus".

Like most clubs, all the lads at Manchester United watch one or the other in our hotel lounge after lunch. It always amazes me how the producers cram so much into 25 minutes or so.

These programmes make com-

pelling viewing, but I'm not so sure I agree with the inquests held by commentators or presenters when a bad tackle or controversial refereeing decision is run and re-run.

Television is so powerful and reaches so many people that the case against the offending player or ref can be built up out of all proportion.

Wherever they appear afterwards the crowd get at them, making it terribly difficult for them to live down their moment of foolishness or bad judgment.

Assists Players

It works both ways. Quite often what appears a bad decision by a ref is proved on film to have been right.

The cameras have also helped players who have been sent off for no good reason.

At their tribunal, film of the particular incident can be shown in defence of the player.

Watching action replays and films of matches can also assist players and referees to remedy faults. Several times I've seen myself on TV and pinpointed just where I had gone wrong during a game.

If I've played well I enjoy watching myself on the telly. But if I know I've had a bad game I'd just as soon switch to the other channel.

Some clubs change their style slightly if the cameras are on them for fear of revealing too many secrets, or dead-ball movements.

My manager Tommy Docherty loves appearing on the telly. He's a natural and finds it easy.

I've only been interviewed close-up a few times so I still get very nervous. I get this fear of making myself look a chump, or saying something I'll regret later.

Manchester United seem to be on the box every week, so cameras at matches don't bother me. I don't even think about them.

I was conscious of them during my Millwall days, though, because TV at The Den was a rare event.

As for commentators, they do a splendid job. They keep up with the play and generally have a good knowledge and understanding of the game.

There are just two criticisms I'd make. Occasionally they get too involved with the play, too carried away and can be biased towards one team.

That's okay when their own country is engaged in European or international action, but sometimes where League games are concerned they appear to subconsciously "support" one side or the other.

I'm not saying they actually root for a team, but you often get the feeling they'd prefer one particular team to win.

Like most people, I'm glad both channels have "sent off" their panels of experts.

Five or six managers sitting in judgment of other teams just didn't work for me.

Continued on next page

They criticised all right, but they weren't constructive. They spent most of the time arguing among themselves, confusing both the programme presenter and viewer.

To be perfectly frank, I sometimes got quite embarrassed just sitting at home watching these "experts" having a go at each other.

It's far better with just one, or two, top soccer personalities giving views on a match.

Having to watch half-a-dozen household names bickering among themselves like kids in a playground is farcical.

Most aggro between the TV and soccer authorities concerns money . . . naturally.

The B.B.C. and I.T.V. pay to cover games, but not enough in my opinion. I reckon they should contribute more to the game.

They put out their programmes at peak viewing times and even sell film of the matches they've covered to practically every other country in the world.

Match of the Day between Manchester United and Manchester City can be seen by 15 million in Britain

The Big Match team at work during a game.

Gordon will never forget watching England's World Cup victory at Wembley.

and ten times that number on the Continent, America, Australia and the Far East.

Soccer players and teams are in the entertainment business and as such deserve a fair payout for putting on a show for all those millions of people.

When Tom Jones appears on the box he's paid several thousand pounds and nobody quibbles.

Show a match like Man. United v. Man. City and the TV people expect it for peanuts.

Having said that, though, our TV is the best in the world . . . a real winner!

I've watched soccer on the telly in America, Holland and other parts of the Continent and their presentation is poor by comparison.

TV has brought me and many millions the very best in sport.

World Cup, British Championships, European competitions, domestic tournaments, the Olympics . . . how else would the majority of people be able to join in the excitement, savour the thrills and the atmosphere?

The presentation provided by both the B.B.C. and I.T.V. is first-class, unrivalled by any other country.

Finally, what about my own personal highlights from TV . . . the games or moments I'll never forget, thanks to the magic box.

My top ten of TV Soccer includes the 1966 World Cup Final. I was 12 at the time and will never forget

watching England beat West Germany.

Perhaps the most moving moment was at the end when Jackie Charlton sank to his knees, overcome with emotion. Like him, I cried with joy for England that day.

Two years later I was allowed to stay up late to see Manchester United and George Best take Benfica apart during extra-time to win the European Cup at Wembley.

Brazil's tremendous 4–1 victory over Italy in the 1970 World Cup Final remains a great memory, so does England's disastrous defeat by West Germany in the Quarter-Finals in Leon after leading 2–0 at one stage.

And I'll always remember Scotland's courageous battle against Brazil in the 1974 Finals in West Germany, when they so nearly won to qualify for the closing stages of the tournament.

Coming closer to home and more up-to-date, I recall highlights of the Second Division match between Fulham and Hereford United at Craven Cottage last season.

Such as the game on a Sunday afternoon late in September, 1976.

George Best, Rodney Marsh, Bobby Moore and the rest of the two teams provided the crowd with 90 minutes of sheer entertainment. Action with a capital A.

Unfortunately, all we got on telly were 30 minutes . . . but a half-an-hour of real magic.

Like millions of others I've watched spellbound as Georgie and Rodney turned on the full range of their skills to help Fulham win 4–1.

Everyone enjoyed it, even the Hereford players who were by no means disgraced.

Players were actually smiling, enjoying the game. There was even one incident where George went back, tackled Rodney, robbed him of the ball and started an attack.

The fun had returned to football and the TV cameras were there to capture it.

Fantastic – the most thrilling 30 minutes I've seen on TV. What a wonderful advertisement for them, Fulham, Hereford and the game in general.

Well, space has beaten me I'm afraid. If I were in a TV studio the producer would be signalling to me to wind it up.

Be happy . . .

George Best and Rodney Marsh have thrilled millions of fans on T.V.

Midlands action as West Brom's Paddy Mulligan
clears from Tony Want of Birmingham City.

A player who has seen service with six clubs could be considered to be a bit of a wanderer . . . and that's exactly what Bobby Gould is.

A Wolverhampton Wanderer to be precise, having rejoined the Molineux club in December 1975 for £25,000.

Since making his debut for Coventry back in the 1960's, Gould has been with Arsenal, West Brom, Bristol City and West Ham as well as Wolves.

Over 300 League appearances with an average of a goal every third game . . . good going by any standards.

Gould's has been a happy career and if he doesn't have a cupboard full of medals, he certainly has more happy memories than most players.

He says: "I've been fortunate enough to play under some of the most go-ahead men in football.

"Bertie Mee, Ron Greenwood, Alan Dicks, Don Howe, Jimmy Hill, Bill McGarry. I consider myself very lucky in this respect."

The next time was in 1975 when West Ham beat Fulham, but Gould saw the match from the subs' bench.

No complaints, though . . . he agreed that Pat Holland, who took his place, deserved his chance.

Gould has invariably been bought to help a club out of trouble. "Bobby'll Fix It", could be his motto. And when looking back he

expense of moving and buying new carpets and other things . . . I'm not in the millionaire class, I can assure you!

"I prefer to think that being with so many clubs has enabled me to make many friends.

"I've sampled different styles of play, different coaching and approaches to the game.

"These things mean more to me than anything."

GOULD'S CLUBS – LEAGUE RECORD:
COVENTRY . . . 78 (3) apps. 40 gls.
ARSENAL . . . 57 (8) apps. 16 gls.
WOLVES . . . 39 (1) apps. 18 gls.
WEST BROM . . . 52 apps. 18 gls.
BRISTOL CITY . . . 35 apps. 15 gls.
WEST HAM . . . 46 (5) apps. 15 gls.
WOLVES . . . rejoined Dec., 1975.

BOBBY GOULD
THE HAPPY WANDERER

Gould is full of praise for West Ham team-boss John Lyall (above) and Leeds coach Don Howe (left).

Gould singles out the West Ham pair of Ron Greenwood and John Lyall, if pushed, as those who have had most effect on him.

"Their ideas about soccer are an example to everyone. I wish I'd been with them when I was younger. I'd have been a better player, that's for sure."

Gould has reached Wembley twice . . . with Arsenal and West Ham.

The first time saw the dream of every player come true as he scored a goal at the famous stadium.

This was against Swindon Town in the League Cup Final, 1969. Unfortunately for Gould, it was The Robins' day and the Third Division outfit ran out worthy 3–1 winners.

can have the satisfaction of knowing that he's always done a good job.

Gould's presence in a team has a two-fold effect. On the field, his experience helps all around him, especially the younger players.

In the dressing-room, his smiling face and bubbling personality guarantee that there's an air of cheerfulness about the place.

Of course, he has regrets.

"I was disappointed when Wolves were relegated in 1976. It was a big blow. I'd been bought to score goals. I had a few injury problems and couldn't really get going."

But the following season, in Division Two, Wolves and Gould showed their goal-power and quickly gained a reputation as the League's Goal Kings.

Only once has Gould asked for a transfer – at Bristol City. So, he has collected something approaching £20,000 in his share of the fees.

"This sounds a lot, but income tax has taken much of this. Add the

'BORO DON'T COPY LEEDS'

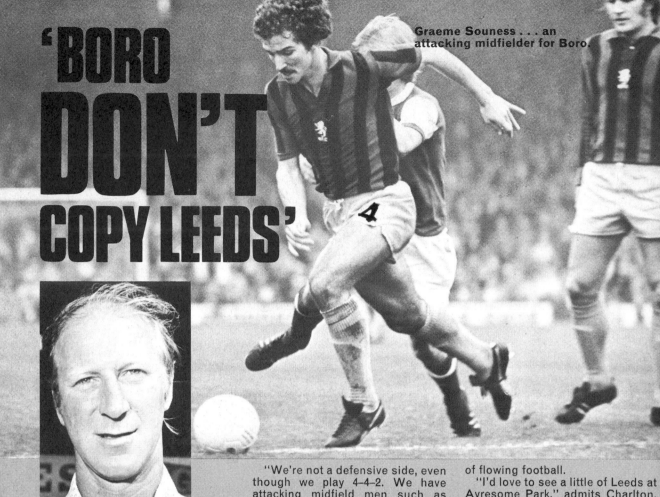

Graeme Souness . . . an attacking midfielder for Boro.

says manager JACK CHARLTON

The Football League has seen many of its colourful managers leave during the 1970's . . . men like Bill Shankly and Malcolm Allison.

Whatever your feelings about them, they are always good for an argument – and, after all, soccer thrives on controversy.

One relatively-new boss who has certainly made a big impact both on and off the field is Jack Charlton, the 42-year-old Middlesbrough manager.

As a player Big Jack was rarely out of the headlines and he has carried on where he left off with Leeds.

Unfortunately for the likeable Charlton, the publicity hasn't been all good and Boro have won more enemies than friends since their return to Division One in 1973.

The lanky former centre-half is man enough to take criticism, although it still annoys him.

Mention that Middlesbrough are boring and you'll be well advised to back away – quickly.

He says: "Only ignorant people call us boring. I reckon we create more chances than any other team in Division One.

"We're not a defensive side, even though we play 4–4–2. We have attacking midfield men such as Graeme Souness and David Armstrong who are forever getting into scoring positions.

"Our trouble has simply been that we haven't had a player who can put the ball in the back of the net regularly.

"It's all very well for our fans to say 'go and buy someone'. On gates of little more than 20,000 we're not in a position to splash out big money.

"I prefer to develop youngsters and search for bargains, like Alf Wood who I picked up on a free transfer from Hull City a year ago.

"He gave us height in the middle and was the target man we'd been looking for.

Revie Influence

"We tried to change our style to suit people but it didn't work. I have a duty to the supporters of Middlesbrough to get results and 4–4–2 is the best formation for the players we have.

"With a little more luck, we would probably be the First Division's top scorers over the past couple of seasons."

Inevitably, Charlton is accused of making Middlesbrough into a Leeds United who, despite all their success since Don Revie took over, never REALLY convinced neutrals they were the team to copy in terms of flowing football.

"I'd love to see a little of Leeds at Ayresome Park," admits Charlton.

"The atmosphere and conditions at Elland Road were ideal in my days.

"If you get these things right, trophies will automatically follow. But I have never consciously set out to make Boro a carbon copy of Leeds.

"Obviously I've been influenced by Don Revie because I worked with him for so many years.

"I'm my own man, though, and have my own ideas on the game."

Charlton, who won 35 England caps, had a long career as a player and made around 800 outings for Leeds before hanging up his boots.

"I don't really miss playing. Perhaps when I'm sitting on the touchline I get the urge to get out there where the action is.

"A manager is so helpless during a game. It's probably the most frustrating aspect of the job.

"I make mental notes of what we do wrong so we can work on these things in training during the next week.

"If management has taught me anything, it's self-control.

"I still associate myself with the players. I have a drink with the boys and play cards when we're travelling.

"A manager can only go so far, and I think I've found the happy medium, even though I would like to be a little closer to them."

my side of soccer

Gerry Francis

'Come training with Q.P.R.'

Saturday is soccer's glamour day, when hundreds of thousands of fans throughout Britain flock to grounds each week.

They enjoy the thrills, excitement, drama, atmosphere . . . everything that goes to make football the world's number one game.

It is, of course, the day players enjoy most of all, but without a week's hard training, Saturday wouldn't quite be the same.

Most players enjoy training. It's not always easy to get into the swing of things on a cold, rainy February morning, but just as you have to work or study at school, we have to apply ourselves to practising our skills from Monday to Friday.

Giving a typical week's training is quite difficult. Firstly, Dave Sexton varies our routines although we obviously follow some sort of pattern.

Secondly, for many weeks of the season there is a game on Tuesday or Wednesday, be it a League game, Cup-tie or international.

Mid-week matches tend to throw training sessions out of schedule. For instance, at Rangers we have had a fair share of international calls over the past three years.

Myself, Dave Thomas, Dave Clement, Ian Gillard, Stan Bowles and Phil Parkes have been on England duty; Don Masson's won a few Scotland caps, while Don Givens has been a regular for the Republic

65

Take that! Gerry thumps the ball towards the Norwich City goal as Canaries captain Martin Peters rushes in.

"England stars of Rangers — Dave Thomas, Stan Bowles, myself, Phil Parkes, and Ian Gillard."

of Ireland for ages.

Being without three or four first-teamers doesn't help Dave's preparations, but he realises it's good for Rangers to have players of international standard.

My week really starts on Sunday. If the match has gone well, Sunday is a nice day and I enjoy the weekend.

I tend to reflect more on a bad performance rather than a winning one, but every professional will tell you that Sunday isn't the same if you've lost the previous day.

Monday isn't a very heavy day in terms of physical training. We go over any mistakes from Saturday's game working on certain points.

If, say, we've conceded a goal from a free-kick, we'll spend time putting this right.

Incidentally, I should say here that

"Sprint training for Rangers — our hardest day."

it is vitally important before ANY training session to warm up properly.

Never go straight into sprints without first getting your joints loosened by light jogging. It's very easy to pull a muscle by failing to warm up before a session.

Tuesday is our hardest day without doubt. We're trained by Dave Sexton and Ron Jones, the Welsh Olympic sprint star of the 1960's, and afterwards all the lads know they've trained hard!

Our sprint-training comprises repetitions of either 100 yards, or 330 or 440 yards.

Try running ten laps of 440 yards with only minimal rest in between and you'll see what I mean!

I can't say I enjoy Tuesdays, although it's a very necessary part of our schedule and keeps us in peak fitness. But it's hard!

SHOOTING PRACTICE

Wednesdays we occasionally have off, depending on how much soccer we've been playing.

If we do train, we will spend the morning at our Ruislip ground working on the next match. This is coaching rather than training . . . there's a big difference in this.

Thursday is another hard day. Shooting practice is invariably on the priority list and this involves all the outfield players.

We train as a squad at Rangers. Dave has the first-team squad of around 16 players while assistant-manager Frank Sibley is in charge of the reserves.

It's important to keep the "fringe" players involved. You never know when they may have to step in, so it makes sense that they train with the established stars.

We usually finish our Thursday session with a game called Five Against Four.

This is good for possession football

Don Masson, Rangers' Scottish midfield ace, shows his style.

78

"Don Givens and Dave Sexton share a joke."

victory and defeat, so we take a lot of time going over them.

We also feature weight-training in our schedule from time to time. There is a huge weights machine at Ruislip, and done under supervision, weight-training is very beneficial.

Over the past couple of years, Dave Sexton has introduced his own system of giving each player marks after every game.

At the end of each month, the player with the most marks wins the Player of the Month award, a watch or table-lighter.

This is taken quite seriously by the players and adds a bit more competitiveness to our soccer.

Dave is one of the top coaches in Europe. Not only is he knowledgeable about the game, but has the ability to get his ideas over to his players.

I particularly like the way he will always listen to our opinions. We may feel we're doing something wrong, or our marking at corners could be improved.

Some managers aren't prepared to listen to suggestions from players, strange as it may seem, but Dave encourages it. I couldn't work under the former type of boss.

Keep reading SHOOT/GOAL,

Gerry Francis

"On the ball during a session at Ruislip."

and the idea is for the Five players to stop the Four from touching the ball. The Four have to see how many touches they can get in two minutes. The game is exciting and played at a fast pace.

Friday, the day before the game, is spent brushing-up and winding-down.

It's silly to have a physical day 24 hours before the match, so we take it reasonably easy.

A few sprints, five-a-side, free-kicks . . . then, more specialised training.

I stay behind to take some penalties against Phil Parkes along with one or two others.

Nearly all the lads remain to do something extra, be it penalties, corners or what have you.

Dave usually announces the team afterwards and gives us dossiers on the opposition.

Some people sneer at such things, but any information about an opponent can be helpful.

It can mean the difference between

68

The Likely Ladies

White Hart Lane wives have caught the soccer bug from their talented husbands and are having a crack at the sport themselves.

They are Anne Duncan (left of picture), Linda McAllister, Sandra Coates, Sue Conn, and Nicky Varney.

Recognise the surnames? They belong to the stars of that famous North London club Tottenham Hotspur.

Their respective husbands are John Duncan (£140,000 from Dundee), Don McAllister (£80,000 from Bolton), Ralph Coates (£190,000 from Burnley), Alfie Conn (£140,000 from Glasgow Rangers) and Mike Varney, the Spurs physiotherapist.

Mike Varney, who has been treating Tottenham players for the past two years, offered his expertise to the girls' team.

Mike, who would willingly have given his treatment free of charge, says: "I would have loved to be their physio, but I wasn't asked. I wonder why?"

The girls play for 15 minutes each way as a prelude to a men's game.

It's usually in a good cause – a local charity or organisation.

On a Sunday last season the girls turned out in a "friendly" to prepare for a hard series of charity games to come.

It proved to be a setback with a 2-0 defeat. It just doesn't seem to be Tottenham's year.

But the lovely Spurs ladies had an excuse for defeat on their opening game of the season.

They were without the services of Sue Conn and Sandra Coates.

Sandra failed a late fitness test with a cold, while Sue had just returned from Scotland and was feeling tired after her journey.

The girls will be a formidable team when they are at full strength.

John Duncan likens his attractive wife Anne to Scottish international Eddie Gray.

John says: "Anne loves to take 'em on and go past defenders.

"But I doubt whether she will make the Scottish team – because they don't have women in their side."

John is impressed with Anne's left foot as he admits: "It's better than mine."

Anne, who plays on the left side of midfield, has been given the credit for making John into a top scorer.

"It's not a case of my giving Anne tips about the game," jokes John, "she guides me.

"She tells me what sort of positions I should be taking up and so far the results have been pretty good – I've scored plenty of goals."

But the wife of Spurs leading goalgetter has got to admit: "I find it hard to score myself.

"I suppose I've got to leave it to my husband.

"In any case he won't let me into the secret. He says he wants to keep it to himself.

"I enjoy playing much more than I do watching football – particularly when John is playing.

"I get really involved in watching John and I become very tense. I can't stand up and scream so the tension builds up inside.

"That's why I've given up going to watch. I'd rather stay at home and relax."

Linda McAllister puts the girls' football into perspective when she says: "It's just a bit of fun.

"I pick up quite a few tips from watching Don, but I can't tackle like my husband.

"I'm a pusher rather than a tackler. Pushing is the only way I'm going to get the ball. I shout at the other girls all the time but they never pass the ball.

"I was playing centre-forward this time although I prefer to play in midfield where I can do more running around."

Don McAllister counters: "Don't let Linda kid you. She wouldn't fetch much on the transfer market!"

Leeds United and Scotland winger Eddie Gray manages to cross the ball before Spurs' Terry Naylor can intercept.

STUART BOAM Middlesbrough

STORY OF A STAR
EMLYN HUGHES
'CRAZY HORSE'

Emlyn Hughes began his distinguished League career with Blackpool. He made his debut in 1966 at the age of 18.

Liverpool snapped up Hughes for £65,000 and he has played a big part in the success story of the Anfield club. Here, he shakes hands with Hibs skipper Pat Stanton (now Celtic) before the start of Liverpool's 12th consecutive season in Europe.

Hughes, affectionately known as Crazy Horse at Anfield, celebrated their record ninth League Championship win in 1975–76.

That same season, Hughes (right) led Liverpool to European success when they beat Bruges 4–3 on aggregate to clinch the U.E.F.A. Cup.

2

3

4

Under caretaker-manager Joe Mercer, Hughes had skippered England. And when Don Revie took over the reins Emlyn continued with the job until Alan Ball was made captain against West Germany in March, 1975.

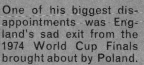

One of his biggest disappointments was England's sad exit from the 1974 World Cup Finals brought about by Poland.

Emlyn could hardly contain his feelings when he went up to collect the F.A. Cup after 'Pool's 3–0 win v. Newcastle at Wembley in 1974.

8

9

Hughes (above, right) proudly displayed the trophy that Liverpool were awarded after being voted Europe's Outstanding Team for 1975–76. Bob Paisley's men had won the League title and U.E.F.A. Cup. Emlyn's fine form during 1975–76 earned him a deserved recall into the England side after 18 months in the wilderness. Alas, for Hughes and England, they lost a vital World Cup-tie in Italy 2–0. (Italy celebrate their second goal, below.)

10

After Liverpool's F.A. Charity Shield win against Southampton in 1976, Emlyn and his lovely wife Barbara dreamed of what the future season might bring.

Waiting for a corner kick . . . Derby County stars keeper Graham Moseley, Rod Thomas and Archie Gemmill. Bruce Rioch (right) is now with Everton.

MERVYN DAY
West Ham

75

Skipper Bobby Moore was superb, so was Bobby Charlton, winning his 106th cap and beating Billy Wright's record. He was controlling the midfield with all his old skill and commanding style.

Suddenly, the pattern of the game changed.

Grabowski was brought on for Libuda and inspired the Germans to surge forward.

After 68 minutes Beckenbauer scored. His shot from the edge of

ENGLAND two-nil up — then disaster!

WORLD CUP QUARTER FINALS TIE
Leon, Mexico. 14th June, 1970
WEST GERMANY (0)3 v.
ENGLAND (1)2
(after extra-time)

England lost their World Champions crown in a nightmare match they should have won.

Leading 2–0, and well on top, they allowed the game to slip from their grip.

Should Sir Alf Ramsey have substituted Bobby Charlton and Martin Peters? Did the pressures of qualifying from Group Three take their toll? Would England have lost their advantage if Gordon Banks had not been forced to withdraw 24 hours before the match with stomach trouble?

Fans still argue over these controversial questions . . . questions which will never be answered.

For over an hour, England were magnificent and fully deserved their lead. They were playing better than at any time during the tournament.

Alan Mullery opened the scoring for England, mid-way through the first-half.

Exchanging passes with Francis Lee, Mullery hit a perfect ball to Keith Newton and then ran to the far post to ram home the centre. It was Mullery's first goal for England – and what a goal!

Five minutes after half-time England went further ahead when Newton, taking a pass from Geoff Hurst, centred for Martin Peters to run the ball home.

West Germany appeared finished, outplayed by an England side looking good enough to reach the Final for the second time.

Alan Mullery scores – England lead 1–0.

the area looked harmless enough, but Peter Bonetti, appearing in his first World Cup match, dived a fraction too late and the ball sped under his body.

Then Geoff Hurst almost settled the issue with a glorious header which beat Sepp Maier but grazed the far post.

With England threatening to add to their score Bobby Charlton was replaced by Colin Bell. You could sense the relief in West German hearts. The thorn had been removed from their side.

Ten minutes from time, Sir Alf made the second of his substitutions – Norman Hunter for Martin Peters.

Before the Leeds defender had time to touch the ball, Schnellinger's high centre caused havoc with England's rearguard and Uwe Seeler scored a freak goal – a back-header that could have gone anywhere, but sailed over Bonetti into the net.

So the match, like the 1966 Final, went into extra-time.

The drama of that Wembley game was repeated when Geoff Hurst scored, but the goal was mysteri-

A near-miss by Geoff Hurst.

76

Frannie Lee, supported by Brian Labone, goes close.

A pep talk from Sir Alf Ramsey after 90 mins.

ously disallowed. There appeared to have been no infringement or offside.

England's spirits sagged after that . . . West Germany's soared.

In the early minutes of the second-half of extra-time, from a raid down the left-wing, Lohr centred into a packed goalmouth.

The ball came across and there was Gerd Muller all on his own, with only Bonetti to beat.

He turned and with his right foot slammed the ball into the net to score. It was practically the only time during the game that he'd touched the ball. But what a price-less touch!

So the World Cup holders were out . . . beaten in a match they should never have lost.

THE TEAMS

England

Peter Bonetti (Chelsea), Keith Newton (Everton), Terry Cooper (Leeds United), Alan Mullery (Tottenham), Brian Labone (Everton), Bobby Moore (West Ham – captain), Alan Ball (Everton), Francis Lee (Manchester City), Bobby Charlton (Manchester United), Geoff Hurst (West Ham), Martin Peters (West Ham). Substitutes: Colin Bell (Manchester City) and Norman Hunter (Leeds United).

West Germany

Sepp Maier (Bayern Munich), Horst Hottges (Werder Bremen), Karl-Heinz Schnellinger (AC Milan), Franz Beckenbauer (Bayern Munich), Berti Vogts (Borussia Monchengladbach), Uwe Seeler (Hamburger SV – captain), Klaus Fichtel (Schalke 04), Wolfgang Overath (1 FC Cologne), Gerd Muller (Bayern Munich), Reinhard Libuda (Schalke 04), Johannes Lohr (1 FC Cologne). Substitutes: Willi Schulz (Hamburger SV), Jurgen Grabowski (Eintract Frankfurt).
Referee: Angel Coerezza (Argentina).
Linesmen: Jose Maria Ortiz de Mendibil (Spain) and Guillermo Velasquez (Colombia).

How They Reached The Quarter-Finals

England

Group Three (Guadalajara)
v. Rumania won 1–0 (Hurst)
v. Brazil lost 1–0
v. Czechoslovakia won 1–0 (Clarke, penalty)

Placings	P	W	D	L	F	A	Pts.
Brazil	3	3	0	0	8	3	6
England	3	2	0	1	2	1	4
Rumania	3	1	0	2	4	5	2
Czech.	3	0	0	3	2	7	0

(first two nations in each Group qualified)

West Germany

Group Four (Leon)
v. Morocco won 2–1 (Seeler, Muller)
v. Bulgaria won 5–2 (Libuda, Muller 3 (one penalty), Seeler)
v. Peru won 3–1 (Muller 3)

Placings	P	W	D	L	F	A	Pts.
W. Germany	3	3	0	0	10	4	6
Peru	3	2	0	1	7	5	4
Bulgaria	3	0	1	2	5	9	1
Morocco	3	0	1	2	2	6	1

West Germany lost 4–3 to Italy after extra-time in the Semi-Finals. But they won the Third Place Match, beating Uruguay 1–0. Brazil won the World Cup in 1970, beating Italy 4–1 in the Final in Mexico City.

after match comments

England captain Bobby Moore:
'I just couldn't believe West Germany had beaten us. I have never felt more confident of victory than when we scored our second goal. Remember we had what was acclaimed as the best defence in the world, and had never lost after being two goals ahead in all the seven years Sir Alf had been manager. It just didn't make sense.

It was a sorry sight in our dressing-room. None of us could really understand what had happened, how we could have been so close to success only to have it snatched from our grasp at the last moment. Only hours afterwards did I realise we were no longer the World Champions.'

Brazil manager Mario Zagalo:
'Like everyone else I was surprised when the West Germans came from 2–0 down to beat England. I won't criticise the handling of the team in any way, but I was baffled when Bobby Charlton and Martin Peters were pulled off in the second-half.'

England team-manager Sir Alf Ramsey:
'We made mistakes and were punished for them. I never thought I would see an England team throw away a two-goal lead and concede the kind of goals we did. After our second goal the Germans were dead.

The players are naturally terribly disappointed but one must credit the Germans for fighting back.'

West Germany manager Helmut Schoen:
'You probably won't believe this, but I never lost confidence in my team, not even when it was behind two goals. We've now beaten the World Champions. We have done much more than anyone expected.'

West Germany captain Uwe Seeler, after playing his 69th international and scoring his 41st goal:
'There was no stronger team in the tournament than England, not even Brazil. Once you've beaten England you know you can beat anybody.'

Gerd Muller scores Germany's winner.

Stoke City's Republic of Ireland forward Terry Conroy (left) is tackled by Sunderland's Dennis Longhorn.

PETER WALL
Crystal Palace

JOHN GIDMAN—
the defender who's a marked man

It's not very often that a full-back is a marked man, but John Gidman, Aston Villa's promising young defender, claims he is.

Gidman has quickly established himself as one of the First Division's top full-backs.

England manager Don Revie has his name pencilled down on his international notepad.

Yet this rise to fame has restricted Gidman's style. He explains: "I used to have a lot of opportunities to go forward and support the front-runners.

"Not any more. Opponents carefully watch for me moving up and put a man on me accordingly.

"Still, in the top flight you don't expect any favours. My attitude is to work even harder to make things happen."

It isn't surprising that Gidman loves to attack. He was a winger at school and it wasn't until he joined Liverpool that he was converted into a full-back.

He remembers: "I was at Anfield Road for two years, but they wouldn't offer me professional forms.

"There were plenty of talented youngsters there at the time. Maybe I suffered from this.

"I was terribly upset when they released me, but looking back the disappointment made me grow up in a soccer sense.

"Anyway, my dad fixed me up with a trial at Villa and they were keen to keep me."

Gidman's career progressed nicely as Villa began to climb their way back to their rightful "home" — Division One.

Then . . . on November 5th, 1974 . . . Gidman's future suddenly seemed very bleak.

A chance-in-a-million accident at a Bonfire Night party resulted in a firework hitting Gidman in the face . . . an eye, to be precise.

Luckily, the club doctor was on hand to rush him to hospital.

For a while, it was touch-and-go whether Gidman's sight would be affected. Fortunately, it wasn't.

He says: "I was lucky. It could have been far worse."

But there was another shock in store for Gidman. John Robson had taken over his number two shirt and, like the team, was playing well.

Gidman even missed the League Cup Final early in 1975 when Villa beat Norwich City 1–0.

"That was the last straw," says Gidman. "I saw the boss – Ron Saunders and asked for a transfer.

"He turned it down straight away and a few weeks later I was back in the team helping them to promotion from Division Two.

"To top it all, Don Revie called me up for the British Championship, which was just about the last thing I expected after events over the past six months."

Gidman didn't play, but Under-23 caps soon came his way and it was clear that he had a bright future at international level.

One of his secrets is confidence, and he says: "A player MUST believe in himself, otherwise he may as well pack it in.

"I always think I'm big enough for the task, whatever the level. I'm not big-headed and have a lot of people to thank for their help.

"But at the same time, out on the park a player is on his own and must have complete confidence in his skills."

Many other people now also have confidence in John Gidman's ability.

'SCOTTISH SOCCER WILL NEVER DIE'

J ust like it says in the song, Scottish football keeps picking itself up, dusting itself down and starting all over again. That is why, like old soldiers, the game will never die.

If you believed everything the knockers told you it would seem that the greatest sport in the world stumbled from one crisis to another and had as much future as Albania's World Cup hopes.

But with a little help from its friends football, especially in Scotland, HAS a future.

Every now and then north of the border it needs a shot in the arm like the re-organisation of 1975 or Scotland qualifying for the World Cup Finals. but talk to the average guy in the street in any city in the country and you will see the reasons for my confidence.

The greatest fans in the world, the ones who turn out at Hampden Park and turn up all over the world to cheer themselves hoarse and lift their team like no other set of supporters can do, take their very lifeblood from the sport itself.

They breathe the air that football exhales and they in turn breathe the life back into the sport. And that applies to those born within the smell of a Parkhead pie and Bovril as well as those who live a hundred miles from the nearest set of floodlights.

Certainly changes need to be made but our top officials know better than me how to legislate for those. I can only speak for the players and it is our job to ensure that we always give the paying customers value for money.

Sell them short . . . and football will have a crisis on its hands.

In the meantime, however, I believe we could be on the edge of a soccer boom. Around 1,000 million people watched

TARTAN TALK
Kenny Dalglish

82

Real Madrid on their way to winning their sixth European Cup Final, against Partizan Belgrade.

LEFT . . . Aberdeen boss Ally MacLeod is jubilant after The Dons has beaten Celtic in the 1976 League Cup Final.

BELOW . . . Kenny (number 11) scores against Rangers.

the last World Cup Final!

That is 20 times the population of the British Isles. And all for 90 minutes of a sport some would have at death's door.

In my book football's undertakers are on the dole.

Even in Italy where the football is just about the most expensive in the world, crowds are soaring and almost unbelievably over the last couple of seasons so is the goals-per-game average.

At the other end of the scale the story is the same.

I remember in 1975 we went to Reykjavik in Iceland to play Valur in the First Round of the European Cup-Winners' Cup and even there, hardly a renowned soccer Valhalla, the game was being re-born.

Helped by British coaches like Joe Gilroy, then manager of Valur now boss of Scottish side Queen's Park, their enthusiastic amateurs were doing all they could to find out about football.

If they treated the visit of Celtic like a royal arrival – and they did – then they seemed to believe that the return of Johannes Edvaldsson, skipper of their national side who had at that point just signed for Celtic, was a re-incarnation of one of their Viking gods.

Nearly 10,000 turned up to watch us play that game – five per cent of the country's population. For a parallel, think of 1 million heading for Parkhead for a Celtic European First Round game.

At home, too, I can't see how anyone can see anything but a bright horizon.

Speaking as captain of Celtic I am glad to see an honest challenge to the Old Firm superiority.

It is good to see the immediate challenge of clubs like Clydebank, the youngest club in Scotland who are bringing crowds back to a once-dead football town and St. Mirren, Paisley's famous old side who are potentially one of the strongest teams in the country.

If the Saints can establish themselves as a consistent Premier League team I see no reason why they cannot have a regular home crowd of around 15,000.

It is up to clubs like them to carry on the good work started by Aberdeen in the 1976–77 League Cup when they beat us in our 13th consecutive Final.

Mind you, I'm not so sure I should be calling that "good work."

But the challenge must come for that is the lifeblood of the game. No Champions, however great, can have it their own way for ever. Brazil and Real Madrid of the late Fifties and early Sixties, Spurs of the early Fifties, Rangers of the early Sixties. All eventually lost their monopoly and had to rebuild.

Indeed my own club Celtic are still going through a period of transition after one of the greatest eras of domination in the history of football.

And that brings me back to what I was saying in the beginning, about picking yourself up and starting all over again.

Sure football, especially in Scotland, has had its rough times . . . but who hasn't.

But it has the strength, mainly given by the Scottish supporters who I believe to be a unique breed, to survive, indeed flourish.

Allow me to quote from the Real Madrid book of football, written nearly 20 years ago. Even then people were forecasting doom for the game in this country.

"If we let apathy get out of hand the professional game will slip into a slow death. We are ready to sit at the game's bedside in mourning and part with a tear for what might have been for football in Britain."

My message to the knockers then would have been as it is now . . . pack it in.

Just as Bill Shankly told Jock Stein of his immortality after the Celtic boss had won the European Cup, I say, "Football, you're immortal!".

Kenny Dalglish

the last line of defence

ABOVE . . . PAT JENNINGS of Spurs, a model for every would-be goalkeeper.

LEFT . . . RAY CLEMENCE in action for England tips the ball to safety.

ABOVE . . . PETER SHILTON shows determination as he rushes across his goalmouth to save during a Stoke v. Manchester City League game.

LEFT . . . DAVE LATCHFORD of Birmingham City is one of two goalkeepers in the family. Brother Peter keeps goal for Celtic.

RIGHT . . . PHIL PARKES of Queens Park Rangers gets behind a full-blooded shot from a Sunderland forward.

BELOW . . . KEVIN KEELAN has served Norwich City superbly in recent years.

BELOW . . . DAVID HARVEY of Leeds United may be English, but has won many Scotland caps under the parentage ruling.

BELOW . . . ALEX STEPNEY has been making great saves for Manchester United for many years – and there are plenty more to come. Alex won a European Cup-winners' medal in 1968 with The Reds.

RIGHT . . . JOHN BURRIDGE is one of the most dedicated 'keepers on the scene. The Aston Villa star often does extra training in an effort to become an even better goalie.

into the net as he fell.

But another goal was beyond the Scots.

So Scotland were eliminated from the contest without losing a match.

How different it might have been if Joe Jordan had not missed a golden opportunity to put Scotland ahead as early as the 17th minute.

That goal could have set Scotland on the way to a victory they so thoroughly deserved.

Scotland undefeated—
but still knocked-out!

Frankfurt, Sunday June 23rd, 1974.
Scotland (0) 1, Yugoslavia (0) 1
attendance 56,000

Scotland HAD to beat Yugoslavia to reach the last eight in the World Cup for the first time ever.

This situation came about because the Scots had managed only two goals against feeble Zaire, while Yugoslavia had put nine past the Africans, and the Brazilians had won by 3–0 in their corresponding game.

In 18 matches overall under Willie Ormond Scotland had scored only 17 times ... and no more than two in a game since October, 1972.

Yugoslavia, needing only to draw to be assured of a Second Round place, gave Buljan the job of stopping Peter Lorimer and detailed Katalinski to halt the aerial threat of Joe Jordan.

Scotland knew the biggest danger could come from the wings, but Dzajic and Petkovic were given little opportunity to shine by full-backs Sandy Jardine and Danny McGrain.

In midfield skipper Billy Bremner was magnificent, but then so too was Oblak.

Inspired by Bremner, Scotland contained Yugoslavia and were looking the stronger side.

Then, late in the second-half, they threw everything into a series of attacks.

Yugoslavia were struggling against the tartan tide. The crowd sensed a goal must come.

It did - in the 81st minute. For Yugoslavia!

Dzajic crossed a perfect ball into the penalty-area, and there was Karasi (a 72nd-minute substitute for Bajevec) to power a tremendous diving header past David Harvey.

Scotland were determined not to go down without a fight ... and fight they did.

With just a minute left, Tommy Hutchison (a 65th-minute substitute for Kenny Dalglish), took the ball to the byeline and his cross was flicked on by Peter Lorimer to Jordan, who slipped the equaliser

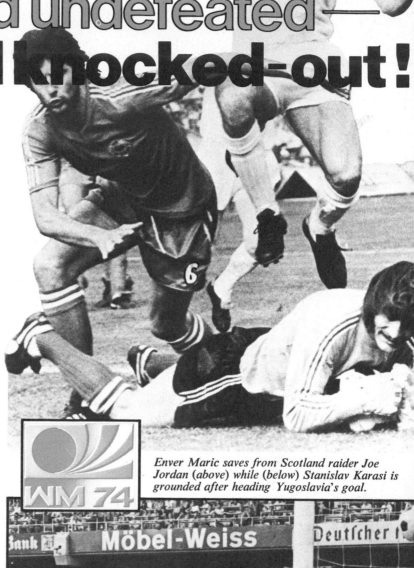

Enver Maric saves from Scotland raider Joe Jordan (above) while (below) Stanislav Karasi is grounded after heading Yugoslavia's goal.

86

RIGHT . . .
Tommy
Hutchison tries to
find a way through
the Yugoslavia
defence.

How the Players Rated
(Out of 10)

Scotland		Yugoslavia	
Harvey	6	Maric	6
Jardine	7	Buljan	6
Holton	6	Katalinski	6
Buchan	7	Hadziabdic	6
McGrain	6	Bogicevic	7
BREMNER	9	OBLAK	9
Morgan	6	Petkovic	6
Dalglish	6	Acimovic	7
(withdrawn)			
Hay	7	Surjak	6
Jordan	7	Bajevic	6
Lorimer	6	(withdrawn)	
Sub.		Dzajic	6
Hutchison	6	Sub.	
		Karasi	8

Referee: A. Archundia (Mexico)
7

Scotland's results prior to their
match against Yugoslavia

Dortmund, June 14th,
Scotland 2, Zaire 0
Attendance 30,000
Frankfurt June 18th
Brazil 0, Scotland 0
62,000

Yugoslavia's results prior to their
match against Scotland
Frankfurt June 13th
Brazil 0, Yugoslavia 0
61,500
Gelsenkirchen June 18th
Yugoslavia 9, Zaire 0
35,000

Group Two
How it Finished

	P	W	D	L	F	A	Pts.
YUGOSLAVIA	3	1	2	0	10	1	4
BRAZIL	3	1	2	0	3	0	4
Scotland	3	1	2	0	3	1	4
Zaire	3	1	0	3	0	14	0

(first two in each group qualified for closing
stages of Finals).

The eight teams left after the
first Group games had been
played didn't contest the Quarter
Finals as in previous tournaments, but competed in two
Groups on a League basis, the
winners of each going through
to the Final.

Yugoslavia competed in Group
B. They lost 2–0 v. West Germany,
2–1 v. Poland and 2–1 v. Sweden.

Here's how the final table looked.

	P	W	D	L	F	A	Pts.
WEST GERMANY	3	3	0	0	7	2	6
Poland	3	2	0	1	3	2	4
Sweden	3	1	0	2	4	6	2
Yugoslavia	3	0	0	3	2	6	0

BELOW . . . Joe Jordan's shot
flashes past goalkeeper Maric and
Scotland have equalised.
RIGHT . . . Joe is hugged by Billy
Bremner.

West Germany won the 1974 World
Cup by defeating Holland 2–1 in
Munich on 7th July. The crowd was
77,833.

87

'Daft' goals

Goals all count the same on the score-sheet – so long as the ball goes in the net, who cares too much *how*? – but, undoubtedly, some are a little more odd than others. Perhaps the daftest League goal of all time came from a GOAL-KEEPER named Albert Iremonger way back in 1925.

A massive man of nearly 6ft. 6ins., he played as the last line of Notts County's defence of a couple of decades – he still holds their record of 564 League appearances – and made himself so popular locally that they even named a street after him when he retired.

He was also something of a comedian – "Mad Albert" they used to call him because of his fooling – but he never deliberately did anything quite so funny as when he was given the job of taking a penalty against Sheffield Wednesday.

The burly Iremonger blasted the ball against the cross-bar with such mighty force that it rebounded to the half-way line before anyone touched it again.

His long legs almost got him there first in the frantic scramble – but a Wednesday man just pipped him to it, and booted the ball on towards County's unprotected goal.

Undaunted, "Mad Albert" went rampaging on – and, at last catching up with the ball just inside his penalty-area, aimed a desperate, lunging wallop to clear it to safety.

Unhappily for him, he somehow sliced his kick – and sent the ball whizzing into his own empty net he'd vacated to take his unsuccessful, action-packed penalty at the other end!

Thirty years later, Arsenal defender Dennis Evans scored a goal just as unwelcome – and almost as crazy.

Well into injury-time of a game against Blackpool, a Highbury spectator blew a long blast on a whistle – and Evans, thinking it was all over, theatrically side-footed the ball into his own net while 'keeper Jack Kelsey light-heartedly applauded.

With a face as red as his shirt, Evans then watched the referee promptly point to the centre circle – as the game still had a few seconds to go!

Fortunately for them, though, Arsenal were already safely 4–0 up before Blackpool got their surprise "free-gift".

Just across London, at Stamford Bridge, the previous season saw Chelsea benefitting from yet another weird goal.

Leicester defenders Jack Froggatt and Stan Milburn both lunged at a loose ball in the goal-area at precisely the same split-second – and somehow their attempted joint-clearance screwed itself into the net

The end-product officially wen

LEFT . . . Aston Villa's Chris Nicholl scored four goals in the Villa/Leicester game in March, 1976.
RIGHT . . . Eddie Hapgood (dark shirt, right) once "headed" a penalty!
ABOVE . . . Arsenal 'keeper applauded an own-goal by Dennis Evans.
TOP . . . Jim Fryatt, who scored the official fastest-ever goal.

88

down on the score-sheet as" *Milburn and Froggatt, shared own goal*" – the only time such a thing has ever happened in the Football League.

Another queer own-goal came only a few years back in a Liverpool-Leeds game – where, of course, there's not usually much given away.

Except on this occasion when, much to the amused delight of the crowded Kop, 'keeper Gary Sprake somehow got into such a tangle that he actually managed to THROW the ball into his own net!

But goalkeepers' goals of the *right* kind, even if strange ones, came when – within three months of each other in 1967 – top inter-nationals Pat Jennings (for Spurs v. Man. Utd.) and Peter Shilton (for Leicester v. Southampton) both scored direct from long clearances from their own goalmouths.

After former England defender Tommy Wright had put through his own net in the first 35 seconds of a local derby against Liverpool in 1972, he light-heartedly bet his Everton team-mates that his boob would stand as the quickest own-goal of the season.

Had there been any takers, Tommy would quickly have lost-out – for the very next Saturday, against Manchester City, he was officially timed as "own-goaling" after only 32 seconds!

Good job he didn't want to bet his second was the quickest of all-time, too – Fulham's Alan Mullery once holed-out in his own net against Sheffield Wednesday less than 30 seconds from the kick-off, and

before any opponent had even touched the ball.

That was just a simple pass-back to the 'keeper which went for a burton – but crazy goals come in all shapes-and-sizes.

Famous pre-war England skipper Eddie Hapgood, for instance, once HEADED one in from the penalty-spot!

He strode up confidently from his full-back berth to take a vital penalty for Arsenal against Liverpool. Now Eddie could really whack 'em but this time his direction wasn't quite as accurate as usual and, though the 'keeper couldn't hold the ball, at least he managed to punch it out.

But the punch wasn't too accurate either – and the surprised Hapgood, still standing in despair on the penalty-spot, found the rebound whizzing back straight towards his forehead.

A gleeful nod – and, even though a split-second later than anticipated, The Gunners got their goal after all!

The penalty-spot, of course, is only 12 yards out – but in 1952 another full-back, Peter Aldis of Aston Villa, scored the longest headed League goal ever recorded.

It found its way into Sunderland's net from fully 35 yards.

Strangely enough, the previous record of 30 yards was held by another Villa man, Frank Barson, against Sheffield United back in 1921.

There was nothing odd about the four goals that Oldham's Sam Wynne scored in a Second Division game against Manchester United in October 1923 – indeed, each beat the goalkeeper all-ends-up – apart from the fact that in this 2–2 draw he scored twice for each side · · · the first (and seemingly only) player ever to do so in a Football League match.

Then, only last March, Aston Villa's Chris Nicholl matched that strange feat at Leicester.

Twice his own-goal mishaps put the opposition ahead, and twice he gallantly hit back to score great equalisers – the second only four minutes from the end.

But old-timer Sam was helped in scoring his "good" goals by way of a penalty and a direct free-kick, whereas the hard-pressed Chris had to sort-out his own chances in the general run of play.

The record-books tell us that the fastest, if not the daftest, goal ever scored in first-class football was that of Jim Fryatt for Bradford against Tranmere in April 1964.

The timing of four seconds flat from the kick-off takes a bit of swallowing – but, even so, it was officially confirmed by the watch of match-referee Reg Simon.

Now, though, the Brazilians are

challenging even that time – and with one which really *was* a daft goal.

They claim our old World Cup friend Rivelino recently did the trick in just 3½ seconds from the kick-off.

Amazing as that sounds · · · even more amazing was the way of it.

Seems the ball was passed to Rivelino from the centre-spot – and, from more than 50 yards out, he enterprisingly blasted it smack into the roof of the net while the opposing goalkeeper was on his knees.

And why? Well, explained the embarrassed 'keeper after, he was deeply religious – and praying he was going to have a good match!

ABOVE . . . "Own -goal" Alan Mullery.
TOP OF PAGE . . . Gary Sprake, who "threw" in a goal.
BELOW . . . Rivelino claims the fastest goal of all-time.

Jimmy Neighbour was feeling very happy. After seasons of being uncertain of a regular place in the Spurs side, he had finally made the breakthrough. He felt established.

His wife had just presented him with a daughter.

As Neighbour was alone at home preparing to visit his wife in hospital the phone rang.

It was Keith Burkinshaw, the Spurs manager. His message was short and . . . well, perhaps not sweet.

"We want to buy Peter Taylor from Crystal Palace. Norwich City

NEIGHBOUR'S HAPPY FAMILY

are interested in you. Do you want to speak to their manager John Bond?"

Neighbour was, in his own words, shattered.

"I had no intention of leaving Spurs, the only club I'd known. I was happy, playing regularly in the first-team. Didn't worry too much whether my name was on the team-sheet each week.

"The phone call came completely out of the blue. To be honest, I didn't really want to leave Spurs."

Then it slowly sank home to the winger that the Londoners no longer needed him. His future lay elsewhere.

"I rang Martin Peters, my former Spurs team-mate who had just been appointed captain of Norwich.

"He told me what a fine club they were and how much he was enjoying his football at Carrow Road.

"More than anything, I was impressed by John Bond. Right away he struck me as being an honest person.

"The way he likes his sides to play suits an attacking player like myself. He doesn't expect me to be chasing back in defence all the time, although I do my share of defending.

"This gives me more freedom in attack and the new lease of life John gave me has worked wonders."

Neighbour was a hit at Carrow Road from the word "go". Which says much for his application because until he found a house in the Norwich area, he was still training with Spurs.

"Even though I knew all the lads, I suddenly felt a bit of an outsider. Their slump didn't help, either."

Spurs hit a bad patch when Neighbour left, including that 8–2 hammering at Derby.

Neighbour will not knock Spurs

or their hard-to-please fans – "They were always very fair to me."

He was 25 when he left Spurs with just over 100 League outings to his credit.

"Things started to click for me when Terry Neill took over. Under Bill Nicholson I was in-and-out . . . always on the verge of being a regular.

"I read in a paper somewhere that I was dropped from the side 16 times in four years. That speaks for itself.

"Wingers are now very much back in fashion, which helps me. I feel my style is suited to the modern game."

Norwich have had a reputation of being unfashionable . . . a soccer backwater. Did Neighbour feel he was "dropping down" by joining them?

"Not at all. Spurs are a big club, no doubt about it. I was there for 13 years in all and liked it.

"But Norwich think big. John Bond has high standards and it's what happens on the park that really counts.

"I have enjoyed my football with Norwich very much indeed . . . even more than I did with Spurs.

"I like to think I've proved John Bond was wise to buy me."

Few Canaries supporters, if any, would argue with that.

1. Jensen's transfer was helped along by former Borussia teammate Gunter Netzer, who ironically left Real during the summer of 1976. The two chat about the past – and the future.

When Real Madrid, the most successful club in Europe, sign a new star, it's a very special occasion. Last year, they paid Borussia Monchengladbach £325,000 for Danish winger Henning Jensen . . . and the "introduction ceremony" was held in typical style.

2. Jensen and his wife Ulla, who was pregnant at the time, can't get used to the posse of Pressmen who are following them everywhere.

A REAL WELCOME FOR JENSEN

5. Jensen is impressed by Real's marvellous collection of trophies.

3. Jensen is greeted by the Real Madrid supremo Santiago Bernabeu.

4. A hotel porter asks for the inevitable autograph.

7. Jensen poses for photographers in the famous all-white strip of Real.

6. Down to business! The Spanish Press "get to work" on Jensen.

8. Jensen and his wife take a look at an apartment in Madrid. The view appeals to them.

9. Time to relax. The Jensens have dinner with Pirri, the Real captain, and his wife.

Two Belgian players who have retired from football, Frans Vermeyen and Rene Goelen, have opened a pub called Elland Road.

The stars were in the team that once beat Leeds 4–0 at Elland Road in the European Cup, and they "want to commemorate the victory".

Australia line-up for the national anthem with their mascot, a toy kangaroo.

Compiled by **CHRIS DAVIES**

THE RISING COST OF REFEREES

Clubs are often criticised for raising the prices of admission for European games . . . but perhaps they are justified.

In the three Euro Cups, clubs keep the home receipts and receive nothing for the away leg.

Travelling is obviously expensive, but clubs also have other expenses.

Police, for instance, don't come cheaply, while officials – the referee and linesmen – are also expensive.

Rangers reckon it cost them £1,000 to "import" three French officials for one European Cup tie.

The Glasgow giants had to pay the return air fare for the three officials, plus travelling expenses to reach the airport at Paris.

Also, Rangers had to fork out an out-of-town allowance plus hotel bills in Glasgow. Of course, while in the Scottish capital, Rangers paid for "internal" travel facilities.

All in all, the Frenchmen cost Rangers around £1,000, but by far the biggest expense to our clubs is the falling pound.

As sterling drops against other European currencies, travelling to Euro games becomes more and more costly.

THIS GAME WAS SENSATIONAL
even in Argentina!

In Argentina, violence on the field seems to be much more readily accepted than in Europe and it's an everyday occurrence for players to be sent-off.

But one match in the Metropolitan Championship made even the battle-hardened Argentinians sit up and take notice . . . a sensational game between Huracan and San Telmo.

Here's how the action went:

4 mins . . Camejo scores a surprise goal for visitors San Telmo. 0–1.

26 mins . Collision in the San Telmo penalty-area. Referee awards a penalty. San Telmo players protest and Minutti receives marching orders. Huracan miss the spot-kick.

57 mins . Ref shows yellow card to San Telmo defender Coronel for kicking the ball away. It's his second booking, so he is sent-off.

79 mins . San Telmo striker Camejo kicks the ball away in disgust after the ref gives a foul against him. Off he goes for the traditional early bath.

80 mins . Sarmiento makes a rude comment to the ref after another dubious decision against San Telmo. Another sending-off.

81 mins . Ref awards Huracan another penalty. San Telmo players don't dare to protest. The same player shoots wide again.

82 mins . Huracan equalise with a Sanchez header. 1–1.

83 mins . Ball goes out of play. San Telmo's Wenner goes to fetch it. A spectator knocks it out of his hands. The ref sends Wenner off for time-wasting. Team-mate Cloquell protests and he's dismissed, too.

90 mins . Poor old San Telmo. To add insult to injury, Huracan score with the last kick of the match. Final score: 2–1.

Valencia fan Jesus Martinez was just getting ready to watch his favourite team in action on T.V. when his wife leapt up and switched to the other channel, refusing to let her husband anywhere near the set.

Martinez stormed out of the room in a rage, fetched a shotgun and set about peppering his wife with grapeshot.

He then gave himself up to the police . . . after he'd enjoyed watching the game, on TV, of course.

Franz Beckenbauer, captain of Bayern Munich and West Germany, with a bronze bust of himself presented to him by a West German sports magazine whose readers voted him Man of the Year.

Spain have already started making arrangements for the 1982 World Cup. The organising committee, which has met five times, has sent a questionnaire to all clubs in major cities asking whether their facilities will be up to World Cup standard by '82.

A publicity schedule has been drawn up and arrangements for world-wide T.V. transmissions are under way.

The Spaniards say they'll be in a position to announce detailed schedules immediately after the 1978 Finals in Argentina.

When foreign stars can't play

At the end of 1974/75, Spanish clubs agreed by a vast majority that foreign players should be allowed to play in the Spanish Cup, from which they'd previously been excluded.

All seemed O.K., but two months later the authorities reversed the decision without giving any explanation.

The clubs were angry because they have to field weaker sides in the Cup and takings are lower when the foreign stars aren't on view.

Spanish players are annoyed that foreigners get more money than they do, yet play less games and have longer holidays.

And it seems strange that although foreign players are excluded from the sides that play in the Spanish Cup, they are allowed to play in the European Cup-Winners' Cup.

The Yankee Stadium, New York . . . 1976 home of the New York Cosmos. As you will see, the pitch is also used for baseball, while in September, 1976, Muhammad Ali beat Ken Norton in a World Heavyweight bout – before a half-empty stadium. This is also the ground where England defeated Italy 3–2 in 1976.

Spain's last-minute subs

*I*t may seem strange to you that a manager will make a "tactical" substitution in the 89th minute, but in Spain it's common practice and nobody blinks an eyelid.

It's not a last-ditch effort to salvage a point or to win the game – it's the manager showing his "appreciation".

You see, in the land of the peseta, where British footballers' wages are peanuts compared with the locals – substitutes can receive hundreds of pounds for a minute's work if you can call it that.

A team may be winning 3–1, so chances are the team-boss will give his two subs a chance to "earn" their win-bonus, too.

That's the way the system is in Spain. The manager keeps a strict rota of subs and sends on the ones who've earnt the least so far during the season.

But even the Spaniards raised an eyebrow when international Satrustegi came on during a European Championship-tie against Rumania and received £2,500 for three minutes on the field!

Thrown into the river

Spanish international referee Sanchez Inabez caused a near-riot during a Burgos-Espanol League game.

Espanol striker Carlos Caszely appeared to scoop a loose ball into the Burgos net with his left hand, yet the ref gave what turned out to be the winning goal.

Angry fans hurled rocks on to the pitch and an after-match "reception committee" gathered to wait for Senor Ibanez.

Unfortunately, a spectator who was leaving the ground happened to bear a striking resemblance to the whistler and the "reception committee" didn't stop to ask questions.

They simply picked him up and hurled him into the river!

In the confusion that followed, the **REAL** ref slipped out unnoticed!

Despair for Tennis Borussia Berlin team-boss Rudi Gutendorf, who has just seen his side lose 9-0 to Bayern Munich in the West German Bundesliga.

JOKE IS TRUE!

You know the old joke about the fan who phones up the ground asking what time the kick-off is and the official asks: "what time can you make it?"

Well, this became reality almost when SC Lokeren played Red Boys Differdange of Luxembourg in the U.E.F.A. Cup.

The travelling fans from Belgium chartered a special train, which broke down twice on the journey.

They arrived 15 minutes after the game had been scheduled to start, but the ref heard about their troubles and delayed the kick-off.

The Lokeren supporters were rewarded with a 3-0 victory.

Similar careers

The careers of two former Uruguay stars, Schiaffino and Ghiggia, have followed a remarkably similar pattern.

They were both in the victorious 1950 World Cup-winning side in Rio de Janeiro when Uruguay beat Brazil.

The first goal was scored by Schiaffino (from a Ghiggia pass) and the roles were reversed for the second goal.

Later, the pair moved to Italy – Schiaffino to AC Milan and then Roma; Ghiggia began with Roma before joining Milan.

These days, the former stars aren't quite so close. Schiaffino is a soccer coach while Ghiggia works in a casino!

Adelardo, the one-time Atletico Madrid star is now on the club's training staff – but isn't paid! The club president is also his father-in-law and Adelardo would "rather work for nothing than have people say I got a plum job by string-pulling."

A trip he'll never forget...

One FC Bruges fan who will never forget the European Cup-tie against Real Madrid is a certain Mr. Florijn who, thanks to helpful drivers, hitch-hiked through Belgium and France.

He then reached the Spanish border at Irun where he hitched down to the Spanish capital.

From there he caught a train to Malaga (Real's ground is closed for three home European ties) but Mr. Florijn's luck ran out . . . all tickets for the game had been sold.

He told his story to Ernst Happel, team-boss of FC Bruges . . . and their enthusiastic supporter found himself getting into the ground on the players' coach.

GERD MÜLLER

the former West German international still scoring fabulous goals for his club, Bayern Munich.

I know that many people were surprised when I asked to be left out of the West German national team after the 1974 World Cup. They shouldn't have been, because I made my decision a long time before and when I informed our team manager Helmut Schoen at the time, the news was well-publicised. Many people wanted me to come back later, particularly when it became clear that with Wolfgang Overath and Jurgen Grabowski "retiring" at the same moment, our

but I really feel there is a limit to what can be asked from a player. For nine years I accepted the time in training camps, playing games and travelling abroad. I scored 68 goals in 63 international matches which underlines the fact that I always gave my best. This is specially true when you realise that in most of those games I was tightly marked, often fouled and nearly always up against a packed defence.

'The best team I ever played in'

national team went through a difficult period. But I never even thought about changing my mind – and have no regrets now.

There were two main reasons for my decision. First, from the playing side I was beginning to feel the strain. Playing for my club, Bayern Munich, we were involved in the European Cup almost every year and always expected to do well in the Bundesliga and the DFB Pokal, the F.A. Cup. Playing for the national team on top of that added so much to the strain and stress that I realised I couldn't keep giving my best in every game, playing as often as I was.

The second reason was even more urgent. Over the years I spent so much time away from home that I felt I was neglecting my family and I wanted to spend more time at home with them.

Most people probably don't stop to think about it, but before every international match the German squad is together for at least one week, sometimes a little more. Then there are the foreign tours, particularly to South America which keeps you away from home even longer.

For the World Cups there is always around three weeks preparing for the competition, and then almost four weeks of the actual tournament, so that at such times you are away from your family for around two months. On top of that we travel around Germany all the time playing club matches and I was often away more often than I was at home.

No one can say that I didn't always give my best for my country

MAIN PICTURE . . . Der Bomber heads a 1976/77 European Cup goal against Banik Ostrau in Czechoslovakia.
ABOVE . . . The Müllers at home – Gerd with wife Uschi and daughter Nicole.

BELOW . . . West Germany's 1972 side – Champions of Europe. The "best side I've played in," says Gerd.
RIGHT . . . Team-mate and friend Franz Beckenbauer.

Of course I have many wonderful memories. Beating England 3–1 at Wembley in April 1972, was one of the greatest achievements in my time, a real triumph, not only for our victory, but the way that we played that evening. Then a little later came the Final of the European Nations Cup Championship in Brussels. I got both the goals in the 2–1 Semi-Final win against Belgium and scored two more three days later in the 3–0 Final victory over U.S.S.R.

That German team of 1971–72 was the best I ever played in, and perhaps the best international team of the last ten years.

The most satisfying goal I ever scored was the third one that gave us a 3–2 win over England during the

1970 World Cup in Mexico. That was my first World Cup and I will always remember Mexico, the people of that country and the excitement of it all. We took third place in that series, beaten out in the Semi-Finals by Italy after an incredibly exciting game that swung first one way then the other. Finally we lost 4–3 after extra time.

Then of course there was the most important goal – the winning goal in the 1974 World Cup Final when we beat Holland 2–1 in my last international. That gave me a dream ending to my international career.

I have always been a little upset that most people seem to regard me as just a goalscorer, a hammer to knock in goals. I've always tried to play a full part in the team game as well as getting goals. But I suppose it is goals that the fans remember, and I must admit I tend to remember them too as highlights of the games I play.

Twice I scored four goals in international matches. I got four against Albania when we beat them 6–0 in 1967. Then I got another four in our 12–0 win over Cyprus in 1969.

I am always being asked how many goals I have scored but really I cannot remember. When I'm asked – as now – I have to refer to record books and ask journalists who keep records of such things.

Six times I ended the season as top scorer in the Bundesliga, including three times in a row between 1971–72 season and 1973–74. Forty goals, 38 goals and 36 goals were my highest League totals for one season and twice I was the leading scorer in Europe.

In one pre-season friendly before the start of the 1976–77 season I scored 11 times in an 18–0 win for

Bayern. And although I had no idea how many goals I had scored, a journalist tells me that I have collected more than 700 goals for Bayern and over 1,000 altogether counting friendly games, internationals and international club competitions etc.

There is another day that stands out in my memory – the day we beat Schalke 04 by 2–1 in the German Cup Final in 1969 – and I was lucky enough to get both goals.

I would never say that I regretted playing football for a living. I enjoyed every minute of it when I was young particularly. But, as you get older you start thinking about life in general more seriously, looking for things outside football, such as family life.

That was why I decided not to play any more for my country, because that takes the pressure off a bit and gives me more time at home.

I look back with many wonderful memories of great games and great players. The players I have enjoyed playing with most were those with whom I was able to strike up a really good understanding. Here I would quote my club colleague Franz Beckenbauer who is a truly wonderful player, and Gunter Netzer who was in the national team with me around 1971–72. Both players have the knack of being in the right place at the right time when I have the ball and need someone to pass to. They also possess an instinct that tells them exactly where and when to put the ball for me when I break away seeking a scoring chance.

At home I have a wonderful array of souvenirs, more really than one could hope for in two careers. In my time I have been fortunate enough to play for teams that have won every honour in the game. The German Bundesliga title and the Cup, the European Cup and the Cup Winners Cup, and at international level the European Championship and the World Cup.

I will always remember with pride the friends and colleagues I played with and many sporting opponents too . . . as well as many of the other kind. But in 1973 I decided the time had come to start drawing in my horns to spend more time at home.

My contract with Bayern ends in July, 1979, and I hope to go on playing for them until then. After that I shall have to see.

Meanwhile I have more free time for my family now and away from football I own two sports goods shops in Munich that keep me busy. Of course I have a sense of achievement at having been successful in my chosen career, but as with all sportsmen there comes a time when you have to quit.

Manager Mirth

"Now I've given you a first-team place, you'll find the competition murderous"

"There you are – stranded in the middle. What tactics would you use?"

"I hope the boss has forgiven me for missing those three goals"

"In the second-half I want you to kick 'em off the face of the Earth – and that includes the referee, too!"

Hull City's Billy Bremner shows the style that has made him such a great competitor during his long and distinguished career.

PROVINCIAL STARS TALK ABOUT
THE OLD FIRM MONOPOLY

Is it impossible for any club in Scotland to overcome the reign of Rangers and Celtic? Will the Old Firm who have been on top for so long stay there for ever?

We put these questions to four of the country's most talented players outside Ibrox and Parkhead and came up with a mixed bag of answers.

YES . . . say wingers Bobby Houston of Partick Thistle and Gordon Smith of Kilmarnock.

NO . . . say the more experienced skippers Jimmy Brown of Hearts and Hamish McAlpine of Dundee United.

And their reasons? Well, read on . . .

'IT'LL GO ON FOR EVER'— Bobby Houston (Partick Thistle)

It seems to me that the Rangers Celtic monopoly of the game in Scotland will go on for ever. And I don't think that is necessarily a bad thing for football.

The history of the game north of the border has more or less been the history of what has happened through the years at Parkhead and Ibrox . . . and I can see no reason in the world why time should change that situation.

Neither club has ever been relegated . . . and make no mistake, such is the power and renown of the Glasgow big two that it would be front page news the world over if either bit the dust.

But the sportswriters can rest easy. The possibility is entirely out of the question.

Empires

When either of the Old Firm get into trouble . . . and by their standards that means completing a season trophyless . . . they have the money to buy their way out.

Consider this. All clubs in Scotland started on equal terms. Some, like Queen's Park and East Fife, have failed to retain the glory they once reached, but Rangers and Celtic built their own empires . . . and more important have kept up with the times to keep them growing.

In doing that they have acquired power and the resources which ensure that they will always have the choice of the top players in the country.

Sure, I would like to see a bigger challenge from Hibs, Hearts, Aberdeen, Dundee United, Motherwell and most of all Partick Thistle . . . but how can we at Firhill expect to break the stranglehold when, in a good season, we are attracting an average gate of about 6,000 while

Partick's John Gibson on the ball against Celtic in the 1971 League Cup Final.

98

four times that number make their way just across the River Clyde to see Rangers?

It can happen of course. Remember that Thistle thumped Celtic 4–1 in the Final of the 1971–72 League Cup.

But that was a one-off. Talking in terms of a real threat . . . a permanent takeover at the top . . . Thistle, Well even Hibs and Hearts have no chance.

Scottish football is soaked in the traditions of the big two. Kids who live across the road from grounds all over the country from Gayfield to Somerset Park, from Cappielow to Shielfield are brought up dressed in green and white or red, white and blue scarves.

Sadly there is no getting away from it. It is a football fact of life that Rangers and Celtic have always had it their own way and in the immediate future always will have.

When Aberdeen won the League Cup last year (October 76) beating Rangers in the Semi-Final and Celtic in the Final, the newspapers hailed it as the start of a new era.

I admit I had to stifle a smile. I thought to myself: "I have heard it all before."

Like when Hearts and Kilmarnock ran away with the League between them in 1965. New era? Celtic, if I might remind you, won the next nine Championships and then when the Premier League started Rangers took over.

Sure, the young pretenders of the top ten will get their chance at the odd League Cup, Scottish Cup or Championship win.

But there are *two* hopes of the Old Firm becoming second-class citizens.

Slim and none!

'GLASGOW'S BIG TWO WILL GET BIGGER'— Gordon Smith (Kilmarnock)

The mixture as before. That, I am afraid, is the way it will be with Scottish football today, tomorrow and for ever more.

In my book Rangers and Celtic are permanent features at the top and there is no way in the world that is going to change.

Our full-time Premier League clubs – Hearts, Hibs, Motherwell, Aberdeen – will always put in the occasional challenge and lift the odd League Cup, but a really consistent challenge, a permanent new name at the top is nothing more than a pipedream.

And I am not saying anything that hasn't been said before when I tell you that the part-time sides – Kilmarnock my own club, Partick Thistle, St. Mirren and Ayr United – have no chance whatsoever.

Success for Rangers and Celtic is consistent trophy-winning. Success for Kilmarnock is staying in the Premier League.

Average Crowds

Willie Fernie, our manager at Rugby Park, knows the limits of part-time football. He knows that it is almost impossible for us to return to the glories of the mid-Sixties when we were Scottish Champions and regular participants in European competitions.

In these days Killie were a full-time club with facilities and opportunities to give them a chance of competing against the Old Firm on almost equal terms.

But then our board took the decision to go part-time and they knew exactly what that decision would mean to the future of the club. However, they were forced to do that as a financial fact of life . . . something that was inevitable when they considered the average crowds that came to Rugby Park every second Saturday.

That move immediately widened the gap between Kilmarnock and Rangers and Celtic and I am sorry to say to this day it is getting greater.

And it is the same throughout the land. Let's face it, the biggest gates for Scotland's clubs are on the days that the Old Firm come to visit.

And I wonder how many players in Scotland, if given the chance, would refuse the chance to join up at Ibrox or Parkhead?

Under these circumstances it is no surprise that the big Glasgow two get bigger while some others struggle for survival. But sadly, that's football, Scottish style.

It is difficult to see how even in fifty years' time the situation will

Continued on page 100

Derrick McDicken of Kilmarnock in action against Rangers.

CONTINUED FROM PAGE 99

change. After all, I suppose it is really the result • of population dispersion.

There are over one million people in the Glasgow area and not even a tenth of that total in Kilmarnock.

Mark you, there could be a chance for us in the future when the population movement from Glasgow to Irvine on the Ayrshire coast is completed at the turn of the century.

I don't expect to be playing then, but with a population in the Kilmarnock-Irvine area of around 250,000 the Rugby Park terracings could be a lot fuller than they are now!

Yet such is the drawing power of the Old Firm that I would not be surprised if even under these circumstances most of the people kept travelling back to Glasgow and Ibrox and Parkhead.

As Jimmy Brown says, it is ludicrous that people pass their local grounds on the way to Glasgow. But it happens and there is no way it is going to change. That's life.

'THE REVOLUTION IS HERE' — Jimmy Brown (Hearts)

The tidal wave of challenge that was started by Aberdeen last year is about to swamp the Old Firm superiority.

I admit that with the resources at the disposal of some clubs, not least my own, Hearts, that threat has been a long time coming.

Hearts, Hibs, Aberdeen, Kilmarnock, Dundee, Dunfermline and Motherwell have all in recent times shown flashes of inspiration and then faded again only to see the monopoly from Glasgow re-emerge. But this time things are going to be different.

The changing times I believe are due to the innovation of the Premier League which has narrowed the gap between success and failure and the gap between "them and us".

New World

These are the vital years. I agreed with Celtic manager Jock Stein when he predicted that Scots teams would flop miserably in Europe in the latter half of the seventies.

But then would come a time of plenty. And all that is due to the new-found competition that the Premier League has inspired.

Competition that must have Celtic and Rangers worried.

The entire standards of football in Scotland has been raised over the last couple of seasons, and while the Old Firm have been improving their standards, the rest of us in the Premier League have been learning at a greater rate.

I disagree with Bobby Houston when he says that the Old Firm have their choice of Scotland's players. At Motherwell, for example they signed Willie Pettigrew and signed him on a lifetime contract despite

the attentions of some of the giants of the game.

And Aberdeen have a side that can boast some of the biggest names in the game . . . most of them signed incidentally after they had made their reputations elsewhere.

It will be a whole new world on the Scottish football scene in two or three years with a set-up more like that of the English First Division where any one of about eight clubs is a potential championship team.

Don't get the wrong idea, I don't expect Rangers and Celtic to disappear from the headlines altogether and end up being annual relegation candidates.

They will still be going for glory with the rest of us . . . but they will only take their fair share of the honours.

That sort of situation will, I hope, change the ludicrous situation of people travelling all the way from Edinburgh to Glasgow each Saturday to watch the Old Firm when Hibs or Hearts are playing in that person's own city.

The Rangers and Celtic power in the past has come from a population situation where, because more people live in Glasgow, they had naturally enough, more people to draw on.

But Edinburgh isn't exactly a country village and if we get the backing of the fans there is no doubt in my mind that my predictions will come true.

Even if we have to overcome the Old Firm before the local support turn to us, then we will do just that.

Aberdeen manager Ally MacLeod, with the League Cup which The Dons won in 1976.

Dundee v. Celtic, 1961. The Dundee side of that era still rates as one of Scotland's best-ever.

If you are going to have a revolution, someone, somewhere is going to have to start it. Aberdeen showed us the way. I am sure I speak for all of Scotland's provincials when I say: "Old Firm, look out!"

'OTHER CLUBS MUST HANG ON TO TALENT' — Hamish McAlpine (Dundee United)

In the early Sixties, Dundee, our city neighbours from just across the road, built a team that still rates as one of Scotland's all-time greats.

They won the League Championship and reached the Semi-Final of the European Cup, boasting a side that included Scottish international players like Alan Gilzean, Alex Hamilton, Bill Brown and Ian Ure.

Our own Dougie Houston was a young member of that outfit too.

But then they broke up and the star players headed south as Dundee looked as if they might be making a permanent takeover at the top with Dens Park becoming the regular home of the Scottish trophies.

Consequently Tayside's fame as a soccer stronghold crumbled and the Old Firm took over again.

My point is this. Had Dundee managed to keep that team together and continued to win prizes, given that success always follows success, wouldn't the country's talented youngsters have wanted to sign for the best club around and thus make the mighty mightier?

We will never know, of course, for the Dens Park men have never reached these heights since, but I think they missed the opportunity for a real breakthrough.

Learn Lesson

The Rangers and Celtic monopoly cannot go on for ever and it only takes one club to show the way by regularly winning trophies over two or three seasons.

If that was to happen – and hopefully Dundee United can be the club to do it – then we would gain the respect of the nation that is currently aimed at the Old Firm.

The 64,000 dollar question of course is "Can it be done?"

Well, it is not easy, that I concede. But it is possible.

Vitally important is to keep any talented youngsters on the books of any club with aspirations to greatness.

At Tannadice we have the most successful youth policy in the country and there seems to be no end to the brilliant players who come through.

Sometimes, as in the case of Andy Gray who was transferred to Aston Villa, pressure is such that moves have to be made.

But generally clubs must learn the lesson of Dundee and try to keep any potentially great side together. In fact, herein lies the crux of the matter.

The great sides of Rangers and Celtic played out their careers at Ibrox and Parkhead and very few of their stars moved south while at the peak of their careers.

Yet think of Hearts of the mid-Fifties (Conn, Bauld, Wardhaugh, Young), Kilmarnock of the mid-Sixties (Forsyth, McLean), Hibs of the late-Sixties (Cormack, Marinello, Stanton), Dunfermline of the early-Sixties (managed by Jock Stein) and Aberdeen of the late-Sixties (Harper, Buchan).

All of these teams were on the threshold of taking over from Rangers and Celtic and then they let all their star players go.

If any club in Scotland wants to stop the monopoly then they must stop the transfers. Difficult, I know, in the current financial climate.

BUT IT CAN BE DONE . . .

When Elland Road fans had no team to support

Herbert Chapman was once manager of Leeds City.

In 1968–69, five seasons after returning to the First Division, Leeds United won the League Championship for the first time in their history.

The following term, they won nothing, except a great deal of sympathy and admiration from players, fans and even their fiercest critics.

Right up until Easter, 1970, they remained firm favourites for the League title, the F.A. Cup and European Cup.

This fantastic treble seemed well within the grasp of Don Revie's team of all talents.

Then as so often happens in soccer, disaster struck.

On Easter Saturday, with six first-team regulars out injured, two own goals and a penalty saw them lose 3–1 to Southampton . . . their first home defeat in almost two years.

That evening, manager Revie conceeded the Championship to Everton – and set his sights on the other two glittering prizes.

But a couple of weeks later Leeds lost the F.A. Cup Final to Chelsea.

After dominating the Londoners at Wembley, Leeds were held to a 2–2 extra-time draw.

In the replay at Old Trafford extra-time was again necessary, this time Leeds lost 2–1.

Before that disappointment they had been beaten in the European Cup Semi-Finals by Celtic, so their dreams of sensational glory lay in ashes.

But Leeds United were too professional to allow past setbacks to halt their drive for future triumphs. They simply started all over again.

By comparison, the disappointments of 1969–70 were minor compared to October, 1919, when fans in Leeds suddenly found themselves without a club to support.

Leeds City, founded in 1904 and elected to the Second Division a year later, were disbanded by the Football League and expelled following allegations of illegal payments to players.

City, in fact, didn't even finish that 1918–19 season (they had ten points from eight games). All their

35 players, including seven internationals, were put up for sale and their fixtures taken over by Port Vale.

Elland Road was abandoned, left desolate and deserted.

Manager Herbert Chapman successfully claimed he knew nothing of the irregularities and was free to lead Huddersfield and then Arsenal through their glory years.

When the authorities hinted a newly-formed club might be considered for membership of the Football League no time was lost, and the following season Leeds United were formed.

At first the new club played in the Midland League but were elected to the Second Division in May, 1920.

Considering they had to rebuild a team from scratch, Leeds United did well in a short space of time – well enough to finish 14th in the table and by 1924 win promotion to the First Division.

But the fortunes of the club fluctuated – relegated in 1927; promoted in 1928; relegated in 1931 and promoted again in 1932; remaining in Division One until they slumped once more in 1946–47.

Leeds United regained their First Division status in 1956 – and lost it again in 1960. A year later the club was in very serious danger of plunging into the Third Division.

Until then, despite a crop of fine

Everton, Bobby Collins.

The tiny genius was 31-years-old, but turned out to be the best buy Revie ever made. His second best was Johnny Giles, for £35,000 from Manchester United in August, 1963.

Then came Willie Bell, Jim Storrie, Alan Peacock, Cliff Mason and Eric Smith.

Such was Revie's influence off the field and the drive of Collins on it, that Leeds saved themselves from the drop. Then in 1963–64 won their way back into the First Division as Champions of the Second.

Apart from Collins and Giles, Revie had groomed new young stars. Lads such as Gary Sprake, Terry Cooper, Paul Reaney and Norman Hunter ... players destined to become household names.

He had also tamed the rebellious Jackie Charlton, at Elland Road since 1952, and a 17-year-old homesick Scottish lad who was always asking for a transfer, Billy Bremner.

The season after promotion – 1964–65 – Leeds were runners-up in both the League (on goal average only to Manchester United) and

LEFT ABOVE . . . Welsh giant John Charles.
LEFT BELOW . . . Midfield dynamo Bobby Collins.
BELOW . . . A great partnership . . . captain Billy Bremner and manager Don Revie. Together, they shared many triumphs.

players like Ernie Hart, Wilf Copping and the legendary John Charles, Leeds had been a club with very little history – and by the early 1960's a doubtful future loomed.

United's first step on the way back to the top came in March, 1961, when a new player-manager arrived for £14,000 from Sunderland. His name? Don Revie, an England international respected for his progressive ideas on the game.

Ambitious Revie, with the backing of chairman Harry Reynolds, set about the task of saving the club from possible extinction.

So great were his problems, that Don Revie even thought about quitting the game.

"It was impossible to sleep," he said. "I lay awake for hours worrying. My wife Elsie and I wracked our brains for the answers. Things were so bad I promised her I'd resign at the end of the season before the job killed me."

Most of Revie's problems were solved for £25,000 – that's how much it cost him to buy a little Scottish international midfield player from

Bremner holds aloft the Fairs Cup after their 1971 triumph over Juventus.

The record-breaking Leeds United squad of 1969/70.

F.A. Cup.

Then they won the Fairs Cup (now U.E.F.A. Cup) the Football League Cup in 1968 and were League Champions in 1969, with a new record of 67 points . . . six ahead of runners-up Liverpool.

By then Johnny Giles had taken over from Bobby Collins as "the man who made Leeds tick" and Billy Bremner was one of the finest captains in the game.

The team was renowned throughout the soccer world – Sprake, Reaney, Cooper, Hunter, Charlton, Bremner, Eddie Gray, Peter Lorimer, Joe Jordan, Paul Madeley and Allan Clarke, a £165,000 signing from Leicester in June, 1969.

Then in 1973-74, Leeds won the Championship for the second time, five points clear of runners-up Liverpool.

In the five-year period between their title successes, Leeds United were never out of the top three and in 1970–71 won the Fairs Cup for the second time. The following term,

Displaying the F.A. Cup, 1972.

Manager Armfield (left) and second-in-command Don Howe.

1971–72, they beat Arsenal at Wembley to triumph in the F.A. Cup Final at last.

As English Cup-holders, Leeds competed for the 1973 European Cup-Winners' Cup and reached the Final only to lose 1–0 to AC Milan in Greece.

But it was the European Cup Don Revie wanted . . . for Leeds and for England. However, he was not to achieve that ambition with the club he had taken from near-obscurity to greatness.

After rumours and counter rumours, Don Revie finally left Elland Road on July 4th, 1974, to become England's team-manager in succession to Sir Alf Ramsey.

Two weeks later Brian Clough resigned as boss at Brighton and

Peter Lorimer in action against Bayern Munich during the 1975 European Cup Final.

David McNiven, Peter Hampton and Frankie Gray established themselves.

Out went Terry Yorath to Coventry, Norman Hunter to Bristol City, and Billy Bremner to Hull City.

Bremner, the inspiring leader, had gone after around 600 League appearances, about 100 goals and over 50 international caps for Scotland.

His £40,000 transfer marked the undeniable end of a fantastic period of triumph at Elland Road. Said manager Armfield at the time: "Billy did a fabulous job for Leeds. I believe he will be of immense value to Hull. Really, it's impossible to replace the existing players with better ones, simply because they've been so great and successful.

"In a sense we're paying the penalty for success and it must be very difficult for the fans to get used to anything but a permanent diet of success.

"People told me it would be impossible to follow Don Revie at Elland Road, and it's been six times more difficult than I imagined."

Under Don Revie Leeds made history in the past. Under Jimmy Armfield they most definitely have an exciting future.

arrived to take over at Leeds. His reign lasted just 44 stormy days.

Before Clough was sacked, though, he spent around £375,000 on three players . . . Duncan McKenzie from Nottingham Forest and John O'Hare and John McGovern from his old club Derby County.

At a Press conference on the day of his dismissal, Brian Clough declared: "This is a very sad day for Leeds and football."

For a while assistant-manager Maurice Lindley took over, but only until October 4th, when Jimmy Armfield was appointed as Clough's successor.

Quietly and without undue publicity, the former Bolton boss set about his new task and took the club into the 1974–75 European Cup Final.

In a disappointing game, Leeds were beaten 2–0 by West German Champions Bayern Munich to end a dream which had begun ten years earlier.

In defeat came disgrace. During and after the match a section of Leeds' fans rioted and the club was banned from European competitions for a year.

The following season, 1975–76, they ended fifth in the First Division after being serious title challengers for much of the time.

Jimmy Armfield more than anyone realised even great teams don't last forever. Changes had to be made.

In came Tony Currie and Ray Hankin, big money buys from Sheffield United and Burnley. Youngsters such as Carl Harris,

ABOVE . . . Frank Gray shows his power.
RIGHT . . . Tony Currie, who joined Leeds from Sheffield United.

Has life 'between

While arguments rage about attacking and defensive football, overlapping full-backs and whether or not wingers will ever become popular again, goalkeepers carry on as usual with their specialist jobs. And to find out if the 1970s have brought about any changes for the last man in defence, Shoot/Goal questioned four Division One 'keepers for their views on the subject.

'Better off now'
Phil Parkes
Q.P.R.

Phil Parkes, of Queens Park Rangers, has never regretted his choice to be a goalkeeper. And in reviewing changes that have taken place in the game in recent years, Phill is convinced the advantages easily outweigh the disadvantages.

"In the matter of protection, 'keepers are better off now than when it was possible for forwards to charge and harry them. There is more physical contact in other positions in the team, and because of this, outfield players can expect to spend more time on the trainer's bench through injury.

"But as a goalkeeper, I not only run less chance of collecting a knock – I also anticipate that with luck, I will add some time on to my career.

"Not that life is a bed of roses for me or any other goalkeeper. During the last couple of years more sides are using wingers, and we have to deal with extra work caused by crosses – and the modern lightweight ball makes a centre harder to judge than it was with the old heavy ball.

"Then on hard or icy playing surfaces goalkeepers are often at risk, which is why I think a match should be postponed if there is any doubt about the state of the pitch.

"Also, forget the notion some people have that we don't train as hard as other players – goalkeepers work at being physically fit and in keeping their reflexes sharp.

"But there's no doubt about it – if I was starting out again I'd still opt for the 'keeper's job."

the sticks' changed?

'Better protected now'

Ray Clemence
LIVERPOOL

"One of the surprising things to me last season was the number of goals scored," says Liverpool and England goalkeeper Ray Clemence. "And there doesn't seem to be any particular reason for it, because teams are basically playing the same sort of game they have played for the last five seasons.

"Icy, hard pitches before Christmas were blamed for some of the high-scoring matches, and there were some unusual score-lines. Arsenal beat Newcastle United 5–3 and Birmingham were 6–2 winners over Leicester in bad playing conditions – but in October, Derby hammered Tottenham 8–2, and we lost 5–1 against Aston Villa in December when the conditions were all right.

"But in spite of these goal-scoring games, I've not experienced any great changes in soccer in recent years. Though goalkeepers are better protected these days, and in five seasons I've managed to be ever-present apart from one week off due to a thigh injury.

"A cheering thought about the standard of present-day goalkeeping in the First Division is that it has possibly never been higher. At least half of the 'keepers in the top flight could be selected for international duty, and Peter Shilton, Phil Parkes and Joe Corrigan are all outstanding in their position.

"A goalkeeper's job does not really alter, and he has a certain number of tasks to do on match-days. To keep in shape for these, I have a special session during the week when our trainer, Ron Moran, gives me a work-out away from the rest of the team and we concentrate on what we think is necessary."

107

"Goalkeepers and outfield players are entirely different in their thinking and attitudes," declares Dai Davies of Everton and Wales. "And in this respect football is the same as it always was.

"Yet there is one change in the pattern today that did not exist years ago – players from defensive positions are more likely to come through and shoot, and to combat these tactics, goalkeepers have to put a lot of thought into their game, studying angles and generally staying on top of their job.

"But a forward, for example, is liable to do things off the cuff, react to a situation through instinct. Maybe because a 'keeper thinks more he is less inclined to make a hasty request for a transfer than an outfield player – but in fairness it must be said that an outfield player usually faces more competition for his place.

"I suppose goalkeeping is a specialist job, and is individual in the sense that in the last resort the 'keeper knows that everything depends on himself. He can have a blinder for 89 minutes then let in a soft goal – and his one mistake is remembered while his good work is forgotten.

"To compensate for this, goalkeepers can have a longer spell in the game than most outfield players, though defenders often go on longer than forwards.

"About goal-scoring – it is too early to say whether clubs are playing more attacking soccer now than they were five years ago. There have been high-scoring matches, but sometimes this happens in patches. For accuracy, results must be judged over the season."

'Defenders shoot more'
Dai Davies EVERTON

'Need to train 'harder'

Barry Siddall
SUNDERLAND

"One thing is certain – goalkeeping is the same in the 1970's as it was in earlier years. But I had to be extra-alert to deal with the sharper finishing of the First Division forwards last season.

"Goalkeepers must have discipline and can't afford to panic – and today I appreciate the fact that I received first-class tuition about my job when I was with Bolton Wanderers.

"Some clubs leave young 'keepers to muddle through on their own. But at Bolton, Eddie Hopkinson and Charlie Wright kept me right – they knew all about the problems connected with goalkeeping.

"And goalkeepers need to train harder. We are diving around, flinging ourselves in all directions during a match, so have to exercise rigorously through the week – and preparation in the Seventies is much more thorough for goalkeepers and the other players than it used to be.

"Lastly, the weight of the modern ball has changed – but although it is lighter than the old one I don't agree with the view that it is much more difficult to judge in the air. When I'm beaten by a shot it's not because I've been deceived by the flight of the ball – it is more likely that the shot has simply been a good one."

One man who is glad wingers are coming back into football is former Liverpool and Scotland star Billy Liddell, whose runs down the flank and strong shooting thrilled Anfield crowds in the 1940's and 50's. His firmly-held opinion is that . . .

'WINGERS CAN BE

Billy, who played in every position but goal in a memorable career on Merseyside in Liverpool's red shirt, is in no doubt about what was his favourite spot in the line-up – it was outside-left.

"I originally went to Liverpool as an outside-right," Billy recalls. "But Berry Nieuwenhuys was first-team choice then, so I was moved to outside-left, though I was naturally right-footed.

"And as it happened, being right-footed on the left wing gave me an advantage. I was able to run across field and carve out shooting positions on the edge of the penalty area, instead of relying only on dashes down the wing.

"So when people tell me that an orthodox winger, who stays on the wing, can be marked out of the game, I have a ready answer – I point out that if a winger uses his brains as well as his feet, defenders will find it difficult to keep him subdued.

"There is no substitute for talent. No matter how much tactics are used, plans to stop wingers like Steve Coppell and Gordon Hill of Manchester United, Steve Heighway of Liverpool, and Ray Graydon of Villa are not enough. They usually find a way through.

"Even when wingers are out of favour with a club, the flanks must be used to give width to an attack and draw out defences – and if a team employs full-backs to go forward and overlap they are simply doing the job of regular wingmen."

The fact that the inclusion of wingers in the Manchester United and Liverpool sides have brought

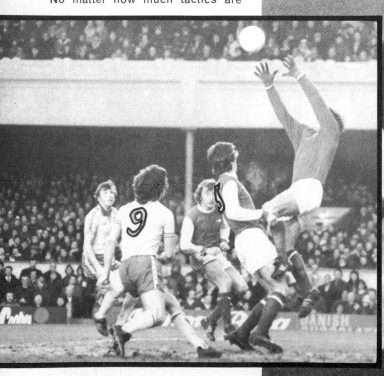

goals and success to the two clubs prompts Liddell to hope that other clubs would favour their return.

Says Billy: "Instead of funnelling extra men back into defence, teams could help to bring about a new era of attractive football if they put a man on each wing. One winger in a front line can make the attack lop-sided, which is why I prefer two up-front.

"This would be a welcome relief from watching games which are dominated by defence – for example, I've seen 21 players congregated in one penalty area during a First Division match when one team is playing for safety. And this is carrying defensive measures too far.

"But if teams are inclined to play defensively, there is no better method of opening them up than by using two wingers. And the way in which two good wingers can

MATCH WINNERS'

LEFT . . . Billy Liddell shows the style that made him such a great winger.
OPPOSITE PAGE, BELOW . . . "Too many high crosses are slung into the goalmouth," says Liddell.
RIGHT . . . One of today's top flankmen – Aston Villa's Ray Graydon.
BELOW . . . Manchester United's Steve Coppell is a real box-of-tricks.

alternate their centres can put a lot of pressure on goalkeepers.

"In today's game, too many balls are slung into the goalmouth in the same way – high crosses that give a 'keeper loads of time to assess a situation.

"We kept them guessing. We would follow a high centre with a low cross, send over an inswinger then an outswinger, trying to keep the opposing defence off-balance.

"Much is said about developing all-round players in the modern game, men who can adapt to any position, in contrast to players who had a limited role in the 1950's. At Liverpool I adapted to different roles when we had players injured, but I still maintain that a good winger is a specialist who can be a matchwinner to his team."

And if Billy were starting his career all over again, he would not change his ideas about where he would want to play.

"I believe there is a definite future in football for wingmen, and with one or two sides now showing a more adventurous spirit, more clubs may look for men to play on the wings – and that is where I would be, given the choice to turn out again. In a Liverpool shirt, of course."

111

Superb action study of Holland's Johan Cruyff, one of the most gifted forwards to grace the soccer scene.

The amazing THOMSON ALLAN

The hushed crowd gaped in astonishment. In the space of fleeting seconds they had witnessed not one . . . not two . . . but THREE dramatic saves from the incredible goalkeeper.

The man who amazed the fans was Dundee's international star Thomson Allan in a League Cup-tie against Hearts at Tynecastle last year. It was the first-half when the referee awarded a penalty-kick.

Drew Busby – one of Scotland's spot-kick experts who rarely gives the 'keeper even a ghost of a chance – strode forward confidently and blasted it with all his considerable might. Allan appeared to go to his right, managed to check his move-ment, throw out his left fist and block the effort. It ran to Willie Gibson, swiftly following up, and he thundered for the bottom left-hand corner.

Again it looked an impossible situation for Allan, but he got across to again palm the ball away. Gibson snatched the second rebound, but as he drew his foot back Allan went down bravely to fist the ball round the post. A breathtaking sequence of events!

"Yes, I was quite happy with those saves," admits the modest Allan, adding swiftly: "I would have been even happier if we had won the game. Remember, Busby and Gibson got their revenge with second-half goals and we lost 2–0."

What the fans might not have known at that game was the fact that Allan might have been a hero FOR Hearts instead of AGAINST them! He was closely linked with the Tynecastle club throughout their re-signing dispute with Jim Cruickshank and his deputy Davie Graham. The man who played against Hearts that day was, in fact, Brian Wilson, a hurried free trans-fer from Arbroath.

But then Allan is used to unusual transfer situations. He recalls: "I signed for Dundee while they were on a tour of Belgium. Then they were in dispute with Ally Donald-son and only had Mike Hewitt as cover.

"I managed to show them enough for them to want to sign me and I was delighted to go to them. I had been given a free transfer at the end of the season by Hibs.

"It was a blow – an unexpected blow. But I didn't want to dwell on it. Looking back now I can realise I possibly wasn't as good as I thought I was at that stage.

"There's no mistaking that ex-perience is your most valuable asset when you are a goalkeeper. Reading a situation and anticipating properly may not be as exciting as the high-flying diving save, but It is just as important – and more consistent.

"Like I said, I was glad to go to Dundee. Mike Hewitt and I had a rare old tussle for the first-team spot before I eventually tied it down. After that I regained my confidence and, after a lot of speculation, I made my international debut against West Germany in a Challenge Game in Frankfurt.

"We lost 2–1 – one of their goals was a penalty – but I was fairly satisfied with my performance and there's certainly nothing to beat representing your country.

"It was a tremendous boost when Willie Ormond told me I was in and I can only hope there are more call-ups in the future. It's an experience I would like to enjoy many more times."

Allan has been one of Scotland's most consistent goalkeepers over the past five years and he is getting better with every passing season.

The man who was thrown on the soccer scrapheap by Hibs has certainly proved them wrong in style. . . .

ROBERTO RIVELINO

At home and at play with Brazil's superstar

ABOVE, RIGHT . . .
Rivelino the father, relaxing with his son Marcio.
ABOVE . . . In the colourful strip of Fluminense.
RIGHT . . . Rivelino in action during a friendly game against West German aces Bayern Munich.

Even among Brazil's glittering array of stars, Roberto Rivelino is rather special. He first caught our eye during the 1970 World Cup Finals in Mexico, but his contribution was often overshadowed by the power of Pele and Jairzinho up front. Rivelino and Brazil were disappointing in the 1974 World Cup, but now the three-times World Champions are back to their attacking best.

A lot of people scoffed when Don Revie awarded Mike Doyle his first England cap against Wales in 1976.

Then another in the British Championship . . . followed by two appearances in the American Bicentennial Cup competition.

Doyle had long been regarded as a good club player, but little else.

Then suddenly, at 29, the Manchester City captain was thrown into the international limelight, fitting reward for the years of honest endeavour at League level.

Few expected Doyle to hold a regular place in the England side – perhaps even Doyle himself – but when England kicked off their 1978 World Cup campaign, the City defender was a vital member of Revie's squad.

Doyle says: "Even if I had just played one game for my country I'd have been delighted.

"To have won a handful of caps is a bonus and must be a blow to those who said I was not international-class.

"When I pulled on the white jersey for the first time, I was prouder than I'd ever felt before.

fessional who gets on with his game without any fuss.

You won't hear him complaining about injuries or looking for excuses if things don't go well and it's this sort of dedication that persuaded Revie to keep Doyle in his World Cup squad.

Although Doyle was new to international soccer, he'd had a fair bit of experience in Europe with Manchester City.

"I learned a few lessons there," he says.

"You get no favours from anyone and you have to earn everything. Referees can make strange decisions . . . crowds can be hostile . . . but it's up to you to put these things at the back of your mind and get on with the game.

"It's no use complaining that the other team were dirty or the pitch was bumpy. If you want to succeed at European level, you've got to put up with and overcome such problems."

He continues: "It was the same when England played Brazil in Los Angeles.

"People were saying how fabu-

lous the Brazilians were . . . how much skill they had.

"I wasn't impressed by the chat and even though we lost to a late goal, I reckon the Brazilians learnt a few lessons from England. People always underestimate us . . . or overestimate the opposition."

Doyle has been captain of City for two years since the departure of Rodney Marsh. Seldom can there have been two such contrasting characters!

Doyle leads by example . . . encouraging his team-mates both verbally and by playing to a consistently high standard.

He's the sort of player supporters take for granted and there can be few compliments better than this.

Don Revie will, no doubt, agree.

Mike Doyle's 'new career'

"It was the beginning of a new career for me. Don Revie was getting his World Cup squad shaped and wanted to use the friendly against Wales at Wrexham as a test for the candidates.

"Injuries and club calls meant he had to change his plans . . . players who were not in the original squad were drafted in.

"I did not mind being second-choice. I looked upon it as a chance to show what I could do.

"Things went well for myself and the other new boys in Wrexham and The Boss decided to give us another chance."

There is no doubt that Doyle is a handy bloke to have at your disposal.

He's a no frills, no-nonsense pro-

Dobson wants more goals

The trouble with being a big-fee player is that you're judged by a different set of standards.

One minute you can be a "really outstanding player", but if someone pays a lot of money for you, you've got to somehow get even better . . . quickly.

This was the case of Everton midfielder Martin Dobson. With Burnley, he was a star . . . a star who had broken through into the England scene.

Then, just after the start of 1974–75 season, Everton paid out a massive £300,000, which made him Britain's costliest player.

A tag which puts you head and shoulders above the rest means there's always a lot of folk ready to knock you . . . as Dobson found.

He says: "Looking back, I didn't realise how much of a change it was.

"Burnley was so near Liverpool I didn't reckon on there being too many hang-ups. I was wrong.

"Burnley are a great club and I wouldn't criticise them, but it's a different world at Everton.

"Everything is BIG and Everton have often paid BIG money for stars in the past.

"I was immediately compared with them even before I'd had time to settle.

"There are always problems fitting into a team's pattern. It took a while to find where I could be used to best effect for the team.

"The Goodison Park supporters didn't quite know how to react at first, although I like to think they're right behind me now.

"They're certainly fantastic . . . they really get the lads to give 101 per cent all the time."

One of Dobson's early games was . . . Burnley (away). A return to Turf Moor just a few weeks after leaving.

"Luckily I didn't ask for a move or anything like that so we parted on good terms.

"I've been back a few times since and I have enjoyed it. I was disappointed when they were relegated in 1976."

Only one thing really bothers Dobson . . . his goalscoring, or rather, lack of it.

He has averaged a goal every six games since he came to the fore

with Burnley and realises that in modern football, midfielders are expected to contribute to the goal-stakes.

"I operate fairly deep, but I should still have more goals to my credit. It's no consolation that many of the ones I score are spectacular long-range shots!"

Dobson faded from the international scene after some bright early performances under Joe Mercer.

Don Revie picked him for the European Championship tie against Czechoslovakia in 1974, but he was substituted . . . and England went on to win the game, his last appearance for his country.

"Football is more than an 11-man game and there is no doubt the substitutions worked in this case.

"I hadn't been able to get involved in the match . . . play was on the other side of the field. Perhaps it was my fault for isolating myself. Still, these things happen."

Dobson, naturally, prefers to talk about the good times.

"I've been at Goodison for three years and I have seen a steady improvement.

"Liverpool's success hasn't been easy to swallow on the blue side of the city, but Everton are now ready to challenge for supremacy again."

JOHN BROWNLIE
Hibernian

BRIAN LITTLE
Aston Villa

FAN-TASTIC

VIVE ARARAT! LES SUPPORTERS ARMENIENS DE MARSEILLE ET DU SUD-EST

Supporters of Real Madrid in full cry (top of page, left). A distinguished visitor to Chelsea last term was the then U.S. Secretary of State Henry Kissinger (centre, in glasses). Russian fans (left) display the banners that let everyone know they are right behind Ararat Erevan.

Two rival West Germans. One with a Bayern flag, the other with a Borussia Monchengladbach flag (above). Manchester United fans with a sense of humour (right).

JESUS SAVES BUT, PEARSON NETS THE REBOUND

Soccer is a kick in the grass

Soccer in the United States has taken off in a big way (right). Surely there can be only one Georgie (below, right) – Best, that is. East German international Jurgen Sparwasser (below) signs some autographs.

SOK, IT TO 'EM GEORGIE

SKY BLUE STARS

COVENTRY CITY manager Gordon Milne was a busy man last August. Inside a few days, he brought three new faces to Highfield Road to strengthen the Sky Blues squad. They were (from left): Ian Wallace (ex-Dumbarton), Terry Yorath (ex-Leeds United) and Bobby McDonald (ex-Aston Villa). The trio have proved to be shrewd investments and Yorath was quickly appointed captain of the club. His midfield drive and aggression make him the ideal leader for the Sky Blues — a club which at last is ready to challenge for major honours.

TIGER TALBOT

ONE of the brightest midfield prospects in England is Ipswich Town midfield ace Brian Talbot. He is a real tiger in midfield . . . a 100 per cent non-stop player with an eye for goals. Here, he comes away from Leicester City's Steve Kember.

Kevin Beattie's good news

The best news Ipswich Town defender Kevin Beattie had for years was that Don Revie had succeeded in obtaining the postponement of League games before World Cup fixtures.

For injury-hit Beattie reckons knocks and bumps have cost him something in the region of 15 international caps.

Now, he knows he has around 10 days to shake off any aches and pains before playing for England.

He says: "It got to a stage when I almost EXPECTED to be injured on the Saturday and pull out of the squad.

"Then, my injuries became more and more. I was really disappointed at missing so many games during 1975–76.

"England went on to the United States and then on to Finland for the first World Cup-tie. All the while I was training like mad to regain fitness!"

Ironically, the man who took over from Beattie was his Ipswich captain Mick Mills.

But when Beattie was fit again in 1976–77, Don Revie had no hesitation in restoring the Carlisle-born defender to the England back-four.

In fact, Revie has caused a controversy with Beattie. Most people consider the player is best suited to a position in the centre of defence, yet the England boss played Beattie at left-back.

Revie denies this is "out of position". He argues: "Only one player is really a specialist – the goalkeeper.

"All others should be capable of defending and attacking as the situation demands.

"Kevin is a first-class defender who is also very good going forward.

"Most full-backs lack the ability to attack with purpose, but Kevin is tops in this respect.

"This is why I have never hesitated in playing him at left-back. Remember, there has been a lack of international-class natural left-backs in recent times."

Beattie does not mind where he plays – "as long as I play, that's the main thing."

The Ipswich star is grateful to Revie for giving him his chance to establish himself in the England team . . . or should it be his second chance?

Beattie, you will no doubt remember, walked out on an England Under-23 squad on its way to Scotland.

He says now: "It was a crazy and irresponsible thing to do. I like to believe I have learned a lot since then.

"I feel more secure. When I arrived on the international scene I felt rather lost . . . didn't know my way.

"I just blew up on the way to Aberdeen and went on to my parents' home in Carlisle. Looking back, I regret the incident but it taught me a lot all the same."

And Ipswich?

"I used to be disappointed that we played so much impressive football yet missed out on the honours.

"But now we are no longer regarded as a small club. No team can come to Portman Road and feel safe.

"Bobby Robson has worked wonders here and I certainly owe him a big debt.

"Without his help and encouragement, I wouldn't be where I am today."

O'Rourke (far left) scores the winner against Celtic in the 1972 League Cup Final.

Lucky Jim— Lucky Motherwell

Celtic just couldn't lose. They were six goals ahead of Hibs in the League Cup Final nine years ago and there wasn't long to go. The Parkhead fans were celebrating on the sun-drenched Hampden slopes – but there was still a piece of soccer magic to come.

The Edinburgh men were awarded a free-kick about 25 yards out and the Celtic defence erected a wall in front of goalkeeper John Fallon. No-one expected any danger to threaten a Celtic team who had swept poor Hibs aside with a sensational display.

But Jim O'Rourke wanted to take some satisfaction from the occasion – and he achieved this with the goal of the game from that free-kick. He curved the ball in a wide arc round the Celtic defenders and 'keeper Fallon was beaten to the wide as O'Rourke's effort zipped in at the post. Even the Celtic players and fans had to applaud that goal.

The next time Celtic and Hibs met in the League Cup Final was four years later. Again O'Rourke was on target, but this time it wasn't a consolation effort. It was the winning goal that took the trophy to Easter Road!

Hibs were winning 1–0 with a Pat Stanton goal when O'Rourke launched himself at a cross from the right wing and goalkeeper Evan Williams didn't stand a chance as the ball roared high into the net. Kenny Dalglish pulled one back, but, in the end, it was O'Rourke's header that was the difference between the teams.

Since then O'Rourke has, of course, left the Edinburgh side for St. Johnstone and two seasons ago he joined Motherwell in a swap-plus-cash deal with Ian Taylor. There were many disappointed Hibs fans when he was allowed to leave Easter Road in the first place – and there are still those who are adamant that his position has never been filled properly.

"It was a wrench leaving Hibs," recalls O'Rourke. "After all, I had been there since leaving school and I never had any thoughts of playing for someone else.

Jim O'Rourke in action against Partick Thistle.

"But after Hibs bought Joe Harper from Everton it was obvious that someone had to go – me.

"I had a good partnership with Alan Gordon at Easter Road, and shortly after I left he, too, was on the move to Dundee.

"I moved on to St. Johnstone and had to start afresh. I had to stop thinking about Hibs and give my all for my new club. I tried my best at Muirton, but unfortunately I couldn't stop us from dropping to the First Division.

"When I was told we would be going part-time I asked for a move and I was delighted to go to Motherwell, surely the most ambitious club in Scotland. I was very impressed by manager Willie McLean. He knows his football and he demands 100 per cent effort from every player.

"That's the way I've always played it so the move was a dream one for me."

It was also a dream move for the Motherwell faithful. In his early matches the powerful O'Rourke showed some superb touches and he combined with Bobby Graham, Harry Hood, Alex Spark and Vic Davidson into giving Motherwell a solid look about their midfield.

He gives you the impression his side could be losing 25–0 with the referee about to blow for full-time and he would still be chasing every ball.

That's the sort of player Jim O'Rourke is. Lucky Motherwell!

SPOT THE DIFFERENCE Answers

1. One floodlight missing
2. Exclamation mark after 'Shoot' gone
3. Boy's arms behind barrier
4. Policeman's eyes open
5. Back's badge missing
6. Stripes on back's socks
7. Lines missing from white-shirted players
8. Stripes missing from his boots
9. Ref's whistle removed
10. Ref's watch missing
11. White tip from his sock gone
12. Dog's collar removed
13. Dog's eyes altered
14. Man missing from crowd on left
15. Goalie's cap gone
16. Teeth changed on player in foreground
17. His right arm changed
18. Letters inserted on left-hand barrier
19. Corner flag gone
20. Support inserted on stand roof

Celtic midfield star Pat Stanton (hoops, centre) fires a shot towards the Rangers goal. Also in the picture (from left) are: Kenny Dalglish, Rangers' full-back Alex Miller, Derek Johnstone (partly hidden), Tom Forsyth, John Greig and goalkeeper Peter McCloy.

Published by IPC Magazines Ltd., King's Reach Tower, Stamford Street, London SE1 9LS, England. Sole Agents for Australia and New Zealand: Gordon & Gotch Ltd., South Africa: Central News Agency Ltd. Printed in England by Fleetway Printers, Gravesend, Kent. Covers Laminated by Oiro Coatings Ltd., using Bexphane Film. Standard Book Number — SBN 85037-354-9